Grief and Trauma in Children

Grief and Trauma in Children provides easy-to-implement, ready-to-use therapy materials to help busy practitioners use grief and trauma interventions in real-world settings. All interventions in the book have been developed and researched with clinicians who faced challenging environments, including devastating natural disasters, and in communities where ongoing violence victimized children directly. Even in these stressful environments, clinicians found the interventions easy to implement, effective in helping children acquire coping skills, and effective in decreasing traumatic symptoms in order to proceed with grieving without impaired functioning.

Grief and Trauma in Children blends cognitive-behavioral therapy methods and narrative practices to present an integrated grief and trauma model that can be delivered individually, to a group of children, or to a family. The book uses the Draw, Discuss, Write, Witness (DDWW) method to help children explore narratives of resilience and build coping capacity, engage in restorative stories about what happened, and reconnect and re-engage in meaningful ways that allow the child to enjoy life again and get back on track developmentally. *Grief and Trauma in Children* also provides up-to-date research on childhood bereavement and trauma, a brief description of the theoretical framework of the Grief and Trauma Intervention (GTI) model, a description of session-by-session goals and activities, case examples with ways to address common challenges, and photocopiable tools for clinicians to easily implement the model, such as session agendas, fidelity checklists, handouts for parents, and activity sheets for children.

Alison Salloum, PhD, LCSW, is an associate professor in the school of social work at the University of South Florida.

Grief and Trauma in Children

An Evidence-Based Treatment Manual

Alison Salloum

Routledge
Taylor & Francis Group

NEW YORK AND LONDON

First published 2015
by Routledge
711 Third Avenue, New York, NY 10017

and by Routledge
27 Church Road, Hove, East Sussex BN3 2FA

Routledge is an imprint of the Taylor & Francis Group, an informa business

© 2015 Alison Salloum

Library of Congress Cataloging-in-Publication Data
Salloum, Alison, 1966-
  Grief and trauma in children : an evidence-based treatment manual /
  by Alison Salloum.
     pages cm
  Includes bibliographical references and index.
  1. Psychic trauma in children—Treatment. 2. Grief in children.
  3. Grief therapy. 4. Child psychotherapy. I. Title.
  RJ506.P66S25 2015
  618.92′8521—dc23   2014033306

ISBN: 978-0-415-70828-9 (hbk)
ISBN: 978-0-415-70829-6 (pbk)
ISBN: 978-1-315-88613-8 (ebk)

Typeset in Perpetua and Bell Gothic
by Keystroke, Station Road, Codsall, Wolverhampton

Contents

Overview   vii
Acknowledgments   ix

1   Introduction   **1**
Current Research on Childhood Bereavement and Trauma   1
Development of an Evidence-Based Grief and Trauma Intervention (GTI) for Children   5
Framework for an Empirically-Informed Grief and Trauma Intervention for Children   10
Steps for Narrative Activities – DDWW: Draw, Discuss, Write, Witness   12
Goals and Outline of GTI for Children   14

2   Getting Ready to Implement GTI for Children   **17**
Environmental Support   17
How to Use This Manual   19
Tips for Facilitating the Sessions   19
Criteria for Participation   20
Abuse, Neglect, and Domestic Violence   21
Critical Logistics   22

3   Practitioner Support   **26**
Worker Stress and Self-Care   26
Trauma-Informed Care   28
Pre and Post Clinician Meetings   31

4   Screening and Evaluating   **36**
Assessment Tools and Evaluation   36
Evaluator   38
First Meeting with Child: Individual Screening with Child   39
Group Composition and Co-Leaders   47
Use of the Clinical Chart   47

CONTENTS

5   Parents and Other Important Adults   **50**
      Parents/Caregivers   50
      Parent/Caregiver Meeting Agenda   51
      Teachers and Staff Education and "Check-Ins"   59

6   GTI for Children Sessions   **63**
      Procedures for Missed Sessions   63
      Number of Sessions   64
      Session 1   65
      Session 2   69
      Session 3   73
      Session 4   76
      Session 5   78
      Session 6   80
      Additional Individual "Pull-Out"   84
      Session 7   86
      Session 8   88
      Session 9   90
      Session 10   92
      Ending GTI for Children   93

7   GTI for Children in Action   **95**
      Common Questions, Responses, and Vignettes   95

8   In-Session Guidance   **106**
      Session Agendas   106

9   Treatment Adherence   **120**
      Adherence to GTI for Children   120
      Adherence Checklist   122

Appendix: GTI for Children Activity Sheets   130
Index   175

Overview

Grief and Trauma in Children: An Evidence-Based Treatment Manual focuses on how to help children who are experiencing grief and trauma. This manual describes an evidence-based grief and trauma intervention called Grief and Trauma Intervention (GTI) for Children. While information on research and theory is included, the emphasis is on providing an easy-to-implement, ready-to-use therapy manual to help busy practitioners use GTI for Children in real-world settings. GTI for Children was developed and underwent research with clinicians who were faced with implementing GTI for Children in challenging environments such as in the aftermath of devastating disasters or in communities where ongoing violence surrounded children who were participating in GTI for Children. Even in these stressful environments, clinicians found GTI for Children easy to implement and effective in helping children acquire coping skills, and in decreasing traumatic symptoms in order to proceed with grieving without impaired functioning.

This manual incorporates all of the lessons learned regarding how best to simplify implementation and incorporate techniques that work in the real world. GTI for Children, a brief intervention, blends cognitive-behavioral therapy methods and narrative practices to help children who are experiencing both grief and trauma. GTI for Children is an integrated grief and trauma model that can be delivered individually, to a group of children, or to a family. It uses the Draw, Discuss, Write, Witness (DDWW) method to help children explore narratives of resilience and build coping capacity, engage in restorative stories about what happened, and reconnect and re-engage in meaningful ways that allow the child to enjoy life again and get back on track developmentally.

Acknowledgments

This manual is the result of working with many excellent clinicians and researchers. The Children's Bureau of New Orleans, Inc. Project LAST, Loss and Survival Team, over the years has constantly strived to provide accessible, affordable, and effective services to children experiencing grief and posttraumatic stress. I wish to express my sincere appreciation to the Project LAST team members and to the children who bravely participated in the Grief and Trauma Interventions.

Thank you also to Dr. Stacy Overstreet, Tulane University, Department of Psychology, who joined me after Hurricane Katrina to continue to evaluate GTI for Children; and current and former Presidents/CEOs of Children's Bureau of New Orleans, Inc.: Paulette Carter, LCSW, MPH; Nina Kelly, Ph.D.; Ronald P. McClain, LCSW, J.D.

This manual is based on three evaluative projects, and the people who assisted with these studies are listed below:

Evaluation Team:
Alison Salloum
Stacy Overstreet
Abbe N. Garfinkel (Project Coordinator 2008–2010)
Laura Garside (Project Coordinator 2006)
Lou Irwin (Clinical Consultant)
Adrian Anderson
Wendy Baum
JoAnn Bruster
Berre Burch
Clarissa Colley
Daisy Cummings
Lauren Eckstien
Anita Francois (Project Director)
Sharon Gancarz-Davies
Lauren Hensley

Tye Kelley
Sarah Larke
Jessica Messia de Prado
Kathryn Moore
Lauren Sampson
Carl Segura
Carlolice Shepherd
Angelique Trask-Tate
Sarah Van Thompson
Mullady Voelker
Stacy Washington
Jill West
Mia White
Carrie Wilson

Participating Schools in New Orleans:
Benjamin Franklin Elementary Math-Science Magnet School
Julian Leadership Academy
Lafayette Academy of New Orleans
Langston Hughes Academy Charter School
Behrman Elementary School
Harte Elementary School
Eisenhower Elementary School

SPECIAL ACKNOWLEDGMENTS

Two of the GTI for Children studies were supported in part by the Institute of Mental Hygiene (New Orleans, LA). We are very thankful for their continued support of the development of GTI for Children and for their commitment to helping children in New Orleans. Funding was also provided by the Tulane University Dissertation Year Fellowship 2004–2005, Fahs-Beck Fund for Research and Experimentation, and the University of South Florida Internal Awards Program under Grant No. R061796.

CASE VIGNETTES

Thank you to the following clinicians for sharing their insight and experience by providing case vignettes to illustrate GTI for Children sessions: Lauren Sampson, Carrie Wilson, Tye Kelley, Shenadra Scrubbs, Wendy Baum, Mia White, Jessica Messia de Prado, and Abbe Garfinkel.

Any identifiable aspects of the case material have been disguised to protect the identity of the participants. In some cases, composite examples were used based on several cases.

For additional information or for training please contact:

Alison Salloum, Ph.D.
University of South Florida
Associate Professor
Email: asalloum@usf.edu

All royalties from the sale of this book will go to the Children's Bureau of New Orleans, Inc.

Chapter 1

Introduction

This chapter provides a brief overview of the latest research on children who experience both grief and traumatic stress, and lessons learned in the development of an evidence-based practice for children experiencing grief and trauma called Grief and Trauma Intervention (GTI) for Children. The theoretical framework of GTI for Children, specific methods used within the model, intervention goals, and the overall outline of the intervention are provided.

CURRENT RESEARCH ON CHILDHOOD BEREAVEMENT AND TRAUMA

While there is still much controversy and discussion in the field about what makes childhood grief complicated, prolonged, or traumatic (all terms with slightly different complexities and distinctions in the experience and expression of the child's grief) (Nader & Salloum, 2011), we know that some bereaved children will experience a loss as traumatic. Therefore, it is important to understand how to work with children when both grief and trauma are present. Some researchers have described the term traumatic grief as meaning that the symptoms of traumatic stress (i.e., re-experiencing, avoidance, and arousal) impinge on a child's ability to proceed with the typical grieving process (Brown et al., 2008; Cohen, Mannarino, Greenberg, Padlo & Shipley, 2002; Layne et al., 2009). For example, a child may have intrusive death images about how the person died, may avoid loss reminders (e.g., places where they used to go, photographs, or people telling stories about the deceased), and not want to go to sleep for fear of having a nightmare about how the person died.

Whether a child perceives a loss as traumatic seems to be more subjective and based on the child's experience, than objectively related to categorization of cause of death. Factors such as the relationship to the deceased; the surviving parent's support of the child (McClatchy, Vonk & Palardy, 2009); the child's level of functioning and coping; beliefs about themselves and the world; and the presence or absence of a supportive, non-stressful environment (Brown, Sandler, Tein, Liu & Haine, 2007), more than the manner of death (i.e., violent, sudden, unanticipated), may lead to a child experiencing traumatic grief. A child does not have to witness death in order for it to be traumatic. For example, Melhem, Moritz, Walker, Shear, and Brent (2007) suggest that childhood complicated grief may occur even in the absence of direct exposure to the death or a traumatic life-threatening event, and the child may experience symptoms such as constant thoughts of the deceased, avoidance of death reminders, loss reminders, loss of security and control, and anger. The loss of a primary attachment figure may be traumatic for a young child even without regard to how the person died (Kaplow, Layne, Pynoos, Cohen & Lieberman, 2012).

Research has shown traumatic grief (Brown et al., 2008), complicated grief (Melhem et al., 2007), and prolonged grief (Spuij et al., 2012) to be distinct from, but associated with, posttraumatic stress disorder (PTSD) and depression. Some bereaved children may experience PTSD in the absence of traumatic grief such that "trauma and loss reminders remain separate; one does not automatically segue into the other, and positive memories of the deceased as well as the pain associated with the loss of the relationship, can therefore be experienced, tolerated, and mourned without interference of PTSD symptoms into this process" (Cohen et al., 2002, p. 316).

When posttraumatic stress and grief are present, there is a complex interplay between grief associated with the loss of the relationship and trauma associated with the death or surrounding circumstances (Raphael & Martinek, 1997; Rynearson, 2001). A child may be experiencing both separation distress due to the loss as well as traumatic stress related to the manner in which the person died or related traumatic elements surrounding the circumstances of the death. With separation distress there is a longing to be connected to the deceased; with trauma distress there is a pushing away from any reminders about what happened and these thoughts become intrusive. Indeed, "separation distress is intent on reestablishing a psychological and physical connection with the living presence, while trauma distress is intent on replaying and avoiding the dying presence" (Rynearson, 2001, p. 25).

Recently, the Diagnostic and Statistical Manual of Mental Disorders fifth edition (DSM-5; American Psychiatric Association (APA), 2013) released criteria for psychiatric disorders and provides guidance on how to diagnose in the presence of bereavement. However, as leading grief and trauma experts in the field suggest, classifications need to take into account the developmental age of the child. Further research is needed on the longitudinal course of childhood grief to help distinguish normal versus maladaptive bereavement and contributing factors (Kaplow et al., 2012). Nonetheless, the current DSM-5 classification can provide a clinician with ways to assess and describe the clinical presentation of a child experiencing grief and trauma.

According to the DSM-5, PTSD may occur when there is exposure to actual or threatened death. Indirect exposure, such as learning about the death or about someone who was threatened, must involve a close relative or friend and must occur due to violent or accidental means. Readers are referred to the DSM-5 (APA, 2013) for a detailed description of PTSD. Generally, PTSD symptoms are characterized by intrusive symptoms, persistent avoidance, negative changes in cognition and mood associated with the traumatic events, marked alterations in arousal that occur for more than one month, and significant impairment in functioning.

The DSM-5 recognizes that when the trauma involves a violent death, both "problematic bereavement and PTSD may be present" (APA, 2013, p. 276). In addition, if the bereaved person has characteristics of PTSD but does not meet full criteria for PTSD, the specification of "persistent complex bereavement disorder" may be used to describe the reason the person does not meet full criteria for PTSD. Persistent complex bereavement disorder is a proposed disorder but was not included as a disorder in the DSM-5 due to the need for additional research. This classification is considered for clinical purposes and for the field to gather further empirical data on how to best characterize bereavement that is persistent and complex and beyond what would be expected in normal bereavement. The proposed persistent complex bereavement disorder may provide a clinician with some descriptive characteristics of indicators that a bereaved child may need intervention. For example, intervention may be needed if after six months the child (1) continues to experience the following: preoccupation with the circumstances of the death and the deceased, intense sorrow, persistent longing for the deceased, persistent distress due to the death (e.g., emotional numbness, difficulty having positive memories of the deceased, anger, self-blame, excessive avoidance of reminders of the loss), and social and identity disruption (e.g., desire to die to be with the deceased, difficulty trusting others, feeling alone and detached, sense of meaninglessness about life, loss of sense of identity since the person died, lack of interests and planning for the future); and (2) these disturbances are outside the realm of cultural, developmental, and religious norms, and cause significant impairment. However, the timeframe and characteristics may vary greatly depending on the circumstances, the child, and the environmental context.

The proposed persistent complex bereavement disorder diagnosis is differentiated from normal childhood grief due to persistence of severe grief reactions for more than six months and significant impairment. The proposed disorder has the descriptor "with traumatic bereavement" for those bereaved due to homicide or suicide. With traumatic bereavement, there are persistent distressing preoccupations related to the death (e.g., about the last moments, suffering, mutilation, injury, or the manner in which the person died) that often occur in the context of loss reminders (APA, 2013).

According to the DSM-5, bereaved children who experience difficulty adjusting after the death may meet criteria for an adjustment disorder, although the symptoms cannot be due to "normal bereavement" (APA, 2013, p. 287). When assessing a bereaved person who may be experiencing a major depressive episode, the guideline is for the clinician to use clinical judgment while taking into account the person's history and cultural bereavement norms to ascertain if the expression is a normal grief response (feelings of emptiness and loss, and preoccupation with thoughts and memories of the person), or if the person's presentation would be better classified as a major depressive episode (persistent depressed mood and pervasive unhappiness, misery, pessimistic ruminations, and thoughts of ending one's own life).

The vast majority of bereaved children are resilient and fare quite well. Generally, resilience is a positive adaptation that occurs in the context of adversity, and, for many children, develops over time (Luthar, Cicchetti & Becker, 2000). Areas of resilience entail competencies within behavioral and emotional functioning, social competence, and academic performance, although how these domains differ based on age and at what thresholds is still to be determined (Walsh, Dawson & Mattingly, 2012). When a child is dealing with both grief and traumatic stress, it is expected that the child will be challenged. Indeed, being resilient after the traumatic death of someone close does not mean that there will be an absence of struggling, but rather, that there are protective factors that help the child to struggle well. As described by Walsh (2003), "resilience involves key processes over time that foster the ability to 'struggle well', surmount obstacles, and go on to live and love fully" (p. 3).

We must recognize that some children experiencing grief and trauma may struggle, but not well. Approximately 5 to 20 percent of bereaved children will develop psychiatric problems and these problems may not manifest right after the death (Cerel, Fristad, Verducci, Weller &

Weller, 2006; Dowdney, 2000; Melhem, Porta, Shamseddeen, Payne & Brent, 2012; Silverman & Worden, 1992; Worden & Silverman, 1996). There may be risk factors or a combination of risk factors that contribute to the child experiencing significant and persistent distress or psychiatric problems after the death of a loved one (see Table 1.1 for a list of potential risk factors). Neurobiological factors such as changes to brain development (Perry, 2009) and stress hormones such as cortisol (Hagan, Luecken, Sandler & Tein, 2010; Kaplow et al., 2013) are likely to interact with these risk factors and place some children at greater risk.

Most theories of bereavement recognize that, due to the complexities of unique situations and capacities, bereaved individuals tend to go through stages of grief or to oscillate between phases rather than go through specified tasks or milestones in an orderly fashion. From a developmental perspective, we also know that children may go through different periods of grieving or have different adjustments to address as they develop over time. For example, Worden argues that the tasks of mourning apply to children but that they must be viewed in the context of the child's development as these tasks may need to be negotiated as the child matures. Worden's four tasks of mourning are "to accept the reality of the loss . . . to experience the pain or emotional aspects of the loss . . . to adjust to an environment in which the deceased is missing . . . to relocate the dead person within one's life and find ways to memorialize the person" (Worden, 1996, pp. 14–15). Recognizing the process of grief over time, Stroebe and Schut (1999) proposed a dual process model which allows for oscillation between loss-oriented aspects (grief associated with the loss) and restoration-oriented aspects (coping with changes) and confronting and avoiding stressors associated with each. The dual process model aligns with GTI for Children in that the intervention oscillates between helping the child to express their

Table 1.1 *Risk Factors for Children Experiencing Grief and Trauma*

Perceived life threat and fear

Association that death is due to action or no action of others

Closeness of the relationship with the deceased

Past exposure to trauma and loss

Time since death

Degree of overall sadness in the home

Witnessing dying, especially when there is physical distress or gruesome images

Pre-existing psychiatric disorder of the child and/or parent and comorbid psychological problems

Negative life events following the death

Child's self-esteem and belief system

Child's sense of competence

Family environment and stressors such as financial hardship

Lack of parental support and warmth to the child

Caregiver's low functioning and emotional reaction to the death, depression, and posttraumatic stress

Sources: Brown et al., 2008; Brown et al., 2007; Cerel et al., 2006; Melhem et al., 2007; Melhem et al., 2012; Stoppelbein & Greening, 2000; Trickey, Siddaway, Meiser-Stedman, Serpell & Field, 2012

thoughts and feelings about the loss and identifying and promoting coping strategies. GTI for Children addresses trauma and loss in an integrative way and provides choices for children so they sometimes can focus more on the loss or at other times during the intervention they can focus more on the trauma. The clinician also helps the child to confront aspects of the trauma and loss experience which the child may be avoiding in an effort to help decrease symptoms and improve functioning.

Children may oscillate between wanting to focus on the loss and needing to engage in activities to distract them from reminders. In a qualitative study with youth bereaved due to the death of a parent, findings suggest that youth wanted to be able to express their loss but also wanted to remain engaged in fun activities (Brewer & Sparkes, 2011). This study offers several key factors about interventions helpful for bereaved children: (1) having a non-judgmental environment where the youth can express a range of emotions from anger and fear to sadness to enjoyment; (2) being active and engaging in physical activity can serve as distraction for some and a way to release or channel intense feelings; (3) maintaining a positive connection with the surviving parent or guardian and also with the deceased person; (4) having experiences to feel a sense of competence and meaning in one's life; (5) having social support and a connection with others who understand what it is like to be grieving; (6) realizing it is okay to have fun and also to engage in humor and laughter; and (7) feeling a sense of transcendence where the youth experiences gratitude and appreciation of life as well as a positive vision of his/her own future (Brewer & Sparkes, 2011). These themes are important to keep in mind when providing interventions to children experiencing grief and trauma.

DEVELOPMENT OF AN EVIDENCE-BASED GRIEF AND TRAUMA INTERVENTION (GTI) FOR CHILDREN

Grief and Trauma Intervention (GTI) for Children is considered an evidence-based practice. GTI for Children is listed on the National Registry of Evidence-based Programs and Practices (see www.nrepp.samhsa.gov/ViewIntervention.aspx?id=259) which is sponsored by the United States Department of Health and Human Services Substance Abuse and Mental Health Services Administration.

To date, there have been four studies on GTI for Children. Lessons learned from each study as well as the outcome data were used to refine and develop the model. Continuous feedback between practice and research helped shape the model into an empirically-based intervention. As the model developed we also looked to theory to guide decisions about components of treatment. Thus, GTI for Children was developed by theory, practice, and research. Importantly, all of the studies to date were conducted in "real world" settings that reflect some of the challenges that community practitioners face when implementing evidence-based practices. The following review of the four studies provides an overview of how each contributed to the development of GTI for Children. Readers are referred to the actual studies for more specifics on the results and statistics.

Study one. In the first study, 45 youth (ages 11 to 19) participated in six 10-week grief and trauma focused group sessions. All of the youth had someone close die due to homicide. Results suggest that there were significant pre- to post-intervention decreases in posttraumatic stress including in the symptom clusters of re-experiencing and avoidance, but there was not a significant decrease in arousal. This study was the first to test an intervention with youth who had had someone close murdered. Several of the youth in the study reported that during the timeframe of the intervention they had other people close to them murdered, and many of the youth talked about ongoing violence. Therefore, we wondered if, on some level, the arousal, specifically remaining hypervigilant, may be protective for youth who live surrounded by violence and who need to "stay on the lookout" for danger. On the other hand, a persistent state of fear and arousal can have profound effects on the brain and other symptoms related to hyperarousal such as not sleeping well, difficulty concentrating, and angry outbursts, all of which have significant implications for decreased functioning (Salloum, Avery & McClain, 2001). Findings from this study led to incorporating more safety and self-calming activities in the GTI for Children model.

Study two. In the second study, 102 African American children (ages 6 to 12) participated in 21 10-week grief and trauma group sessions that were conducted in schools, afterschool programs, and community centers. Eighty-nine children reported that they had someone close to them die due to homicide, and the other children reported exposure to community violence. Similar to the first study (which was with adolescents), there was a significant decrease in post-traumatic stress from pre- to post-intervention, with significant decreases in re-experiencing and avoidance, but again not for arousal. While there was a 34 percent decrease in children who scored within the clinical range for likely PTSD, 37 children continued to score in the clinical range, and the effect size (a standardized statistic to report the difference between two means) was moderate ($d = .49$) (Salloum, 2008).

There were several lessons learned from the second study that led to changes in the GTI for Children model to improve the intervention. These changes included:

1. A parent/caregiver component was added so that at least one meeting with the parent/caregiver occurs.
2. A structured pre-intervention screening process was developed to learn more about the child and to assess the appropriateness of GTI for Children for each child.
3. Gender-specific groups for preadolescents, when possible, are recommended.
4. Children in group treatment who witnessed the death may also need individual or family treatment.
5. A fidelity checklist was created to ensure that the essentials of GTI for Children are provided.
6. The model was designed to be completed within 10 weeks. When groups are provided in school settings, it is recommended that the intervention be completed within one semester and not be provided when there are long breaks such that the treatment starts, stops, and starts again.
7. Anger management was included in the first three sessions to help children manage their behavior and reduce school suspensions.
8. When GTI for Children is provided in a group setting, a "pull-out" session (i.e., an individualized session) similar to the approach developed by March, Amaya-Jackson, Murray, and Schulte (1998) was included to address the unique needs of each child and to provide individualized interventions focusing on decreasing traumatic stress.
9. A missed session protocol was developed to ensure children receive the entire intervention.

10. To target arousal symptoms, three topics related to safety (ways to feel safe, creating a safe place, and teaching relaxation) were included in the model and relaxation was practiced throughout the intervention.

11. An activity specifically related to dreams and nightmares was included. In addition, if the child continues to have difficulty sleeping, an additional session with the parent should occur to discuss this issue and problem-solve (Salloum, 2008).

Study three. In 2005, we incorporated changes from the second study and planned to conduct another study on the revised GTI for Children model. In the fall of 2005 we started the third study on GTI for Children. Right after we sent consent forms to parents in four elementary schools for permission for their children to participate in the GTI for Children study, Hurricane Katrina hit the area. Hurricane Katrina was one of the most destructive hurricanes in the history of the United States. The four schools that were identified to take part in the study were severely damaged.

The semester was cancelled and four months after the storm some schools in a non-flooded area of the city opened. We identified new schools and began the third study on GTI for Children. We decided that since GTI for Children had been pilot tested in the area with African American children and promising results were obtained, we could continue to use GTI for Children after the disaster. We also knew that the intervention with these children needed to address the stress related to the storm, and to address trauma and losses that occurred prior to the storm. As some of the locals said, the storm brought new stress but did not wash away the pain and loss of the past. We revised GTI for Children to address disaster-related grief and loss and to include ways to help children with multiple losses and traumas.

GTI for Children had been developed as a group model but we wondered if children who were experiencing stress due to disaster might have better outcomes receiving individual therapy. But we also considered that group therapy allows more children to be provided with the intervention with less therapist time and, given the magnitude of the need for intervention, group therapy may have been a better format so that more children could receive care (Salloum, Garfield, Irwin, Anderson & Francois, 2009). We designed the study to compare GTI for Children provided individually versus GTI for Children provided in a group format. The GTI for Children manual was revised to offer tips for providing the intervention individually rather than just in a group setting. In addition to measuring changes in PTSD, we included measures of depression, traumatic grief, and global distress, and we examined treatment satisfaction. Findings suggested that there were significant decreases in all outcome measures over time (pre, post, and three-week follow-up), and there were no differences in outcomes between children who participated in GTI for Children individually or within a group setting. From pre-treatment to post-treatment, there was a 75 percent decrease of children who scored within the clinical range for likely PTSD. Twenty-four children were in the clinical range before treatment whereas only six were in the clinical range at post-assessment and only two children were in the clinical range during the follow-up assessment. The effect size from pre- to post-intervention was much higher than in the previous trial ($d = 1.16$ at post-assessment and $d = 1.82$ at follow-up) (Salloum & Overstreet, 2008).

We decided against using a control group or wait-list group in the study since the intervention was to be provided during the spring semester and we would not be able to provide the intervention to these children in the summer. Without a control group, there are limitations such as not being able to control for the passage of time as the reason children improved. However, we are able to examine previous research on the natural decrease in PTSD in children after a hurricane. The symptom decrease in this GTI for Children study post-Hurricane Katrina is larger than those observed in longitudinal studies of the course of posttraumatic distress post-hurricane (La Greca, Silverman, Vernberg & Prinstein, 1996; Shaw et al., 1995). For example, LaGreca and associates (1996) found of the children (129) with severe or very severe levels of PTSD (i.e., in the clinical range) following Hurricane Andrew, there was a 37 percent improvement from 3 months to 7 months. In this GTI for Children study, there was a 75 to 92 percent improvement in children no longer above the PTSD clinical cutoff score from 4.5 months to 8–9 months later.

Of the team that had been trained before the storm to conduct the GTI for Children study, only the researcher (author of this book) and one clinician returned to the city in the immediate aftermath of Hurricane Katrina. Therefore, one of the major challenges conducting the third study on GTI for Children post-Hurricane Katrina was that five of the six clinicians had never implemented GTI for Children and had to be quickly trained. In addition, the clinicians and researchers themselves were affected by the storm and many were experiencing hardships such as having had their homes destroyed; living in crowded homes with friends, relatives, or in hotels; being separated from family and friends; loss of income; and the added stress of living in a post-disaster environment. During weekly consultation meetings, the team discussed the difficulty of hearing about the magnitude of the trauma and loss that the children had experienced, while at the same time struggling with their own stress. Indeed, "shared traumatic reality," that is, after a catastrophe the professional experiences dual exposure to trauma resulting from their own (primary) and those with whom they are working (secondary) (Baum, 2012; Tosone, Nuttman-Shwartz & Stephens, 2012), was very present for the clinicians. Nevertheless, we were able to conduct a rigorous study despite the many challenges to implementing treatment research in a post-disaster environment. In this study, we employed several of the "gold standards" of trauma treatment research such as clearly defined goals, standardized measures, blind evaluators, assessor training, manualized treatment, trained clinicians in both modalities, randomized treatment assignment and therapist assignment, treatment adherence, and an intent-to-treat analysis. A major strength of this study is that it was conducted in a "real world" setting in a post-disaster environment that was still very unstable.

Given the difficulty of training clinicians to implement evidence-based practices along with added stress of shared trauma, we considered developing a GTI for Children model that focuses on coping skills and without the trauma narrative component, which may be easier to train clinicians to use. In fact, a recent study with 103 child advocacy center clinicians who are trained in trauma-focused cognitive behavioral therapy (TF-CBT) found that clinicians preferred delivering the skill building techniques more than the trauma narrative (Allen & Johnson, 2012).

Study four. The fourth study on GTI for Children compared the standard GTI for Children intervention with the trauma narrative (GTI-CTN) to GTI for Children with coping skills only (GTI-C). In preparation for this study, we made sure the trauma narrative sessions in GTI for Children included clearly structured processes for helping the clinician facilitate the trauma and loss narrative components with the child, and that GTI-C did not incorporate structured processing of the trauma or loss narrative. The trauma narrative is considered a type of exposure to the trauma which has been recommended as an important aspect of effective treatment for childhood trauma (Foa, Keane, Friedman & Cohen, 2009). Both GTI for Children interventions followed the same format with 10 group sessions, one individual session, and at least one meeting with the parent/caregiver. The GTI-C manual included all of the coping skills activities addressed in GTI-CTN, with these skills being reinforced in place of processing the trauma loss narrative. In addition to including manualized treatments, blind evaluators, standardized measures, and child self-reports (all methods used in previous studies), we also included 3- and 12-month follow-up as well as parent reports of children's behavior.

Three years post-Hurricane Katrina, 70 African American children (ages 7 to 12) participated in a school-based randomized clinical trial group treatment with GTI for Children with and without the structured trauma and loss narrative components. Similar to the other studies, the clinical trial took place in New Orleans. Right after the consent forms were sent to parents, another hurricane (Hurricane Gustav) threatened to hit the city, causing a massive mandatory evacuation of all residents, leading to a week-long closure of the schools. The hurricane landed miles away from the study area but still caused anxiety and disruption to the children and families. Once children returned to the city, we had to redistribute the consent forms and start the pre-screenings for participation in the GTI for Children groups. The assessments for this study occurred right after the third anniversary of Hurricane Katrina (Salloum & Overstreet, 2012).

When we began this study we wondered how exposure to the approach of Hurricane Gustav affected the levels of posttraumatic stress (PTSS) and depression symptoms in the children and if any increase in symptoms would depend on prior exposure to Hurricane Katrina or prior exposure to community violence. Using data from all of the children who underwent a pre-screening (122), we found that exposure to Hurricane Gustav was not associated with increased symptoms of PTSS and depression, but the relationship between exposure to Hurricane Gustav and symptoms was moderated by prior experiences. As such, for children who had *either* high exposure to Hurricane Katrina or high exposure to community violence, there was a positive relationship between exposure to Hurricane Gustav and PTSS. There was no relationship between Gustav exposure and PTSS for children with low Katrina exposure and low exposure to community violence or for children with high Katrina exposure *and* high exposure to community violence. The relationship between exposure to Gustav and depression was not moderated by children's prior experience (Salloum, Carter, Burch, Garfinkel & Overstreet, 2011).

In essence, prior high exposure to either Hurricane Katrina or community violence amplified the relationship between exposure to Hurricane Gustav and PTSS for children, but when the cumulativeness of high exposures to both Katrina and community violence was present there was no relationship between Gustav and PTSS, suggesting that children with high cumulative exposure did not experience a rapid increase of symptoms. These children with high levels of previous exposure to disaster and violence may have not increased in symptoms after Hurricane Gustav because they were already at the high end of being symptomatic or maybe because they did not view Gustav as traumatic, especially compared to their other experiences (Salloum et al., 2011). From a clinical standpoint, this study informed us that we did not need to add a major focus on the impact of Hurricane Gustav in the current intervention study as not all children were impacted symptomatically by the "near miss" disaster. Also, this experience with another potentially traumatic event stressed the importance of having a flexible intervention model that can address multiple traumas and losses and also target those events that may be causing the most distress.

Results for the GTI-CTN versus GTI-C study suggested that both treatments were effective in decreasing distress-related symptoms and increasing social support and, with the exception of externalizing symptoms in the GTI-C group, these improvements were maintained at the 12-month follow-up. However, it was noted that effect sizes, the percentage classified as improvers and those classified as deteriorating, and the percentage of children who were no longer within the clinical levels were lower for the GTI-CTN group that had the structured trauma and loss processing. Therefore, while GTI-C seems to be a viable intervention, we suggest that the coping plus narrative component may be more beneficial for children, especially those experiencing high levels of distress (Salloum & Overstreet, 2012). Other studies testing the use of child trauma-focused models with and without trauma narratives (Deblinger, Mannarino, Cohen, Runyon & Steer, 2010) and CBT with and without exposure (Nixon, Sterk & Pearce, 2012) have found similar results, suggesting that the narrative/exposure component may not be necessary for all children to experience decrease in symptoms, but better outcomes or more improvements have been found when the narrative/exposure component is included. Until we know which children need which components of specific interventions (i.e., more coping or more narrative/exposure), we recommend the use of both coping and narrative exposure for children experiencing grief and traumatic stress. Thus, the GTI for Children model described in this book includes promoting coping skills and processing in the trauma and loss narrative. Findings from this study (Salloum & Overstreet, 2012) also supported that parents recognized the improvements in children participating in GTI for Children and that improvements from a short-term grief and trauma-focused intervention can be maintained over time.

FRAMEWORK FOR AN EMPIRICALLY-INFORMED GRIEF AND TRAUMA INTERVENTION FOR CHILDREN

Because the intention of this book is to provide an evidence-based treatment manual rather than long descriptions of research studies and theory, this section will briefly highlight the theoretical underpinnings of this model and assume that the user is informed about these theories. Table 1.2 provides an overview of the main theories supporting GTI for Children as well as the themes addressed within each section.

The foundation of GTI for Children is based on what we call *DEC: developmentally specific interventions*, an *ecological perspective*, and *culturally relevant methods*. In addition, the ordering of session objectives and themes is based on three overlapping phases: (1) *resilience and safety*; (2) *restorative retelling*; and (3) *reconnecting* (Herman, 1997; Rynearson, 2001). The ordering is also congruent with *group development theory* where there is time for orientation, time working toward more cohesion and mutual support, and then time for preparing group members for separation and termination (Northen & Kurland, 2001). The practice theories used to implement the activities are based on *cognitive behavioral therapy* (CBT; March et al., 1998) and *narrative therapy* (White, 2007).

The intervention is designed to be *developmentally specific* with an activity-based approach utilizing art, drama, and play. Topics that are common to elementary-school-age children who are experiencing grief and trauma are included, such as dreams (nightmares), questioning, anger, and guilt. Clinicians should try to tailor the intervention to be as developmentally specific as possible. For example, younger children may require more one-to-one time and may need to have more calming activities included such as coloring and use of puppets or storytelling; older children may want to write more or have more discussion.

GTI for Children is to be conducted within the ecological paradigm. The *ecological perspective* provides a framework for understanding the child and considers the environmental context as well as the bi-directional processes which occur within and between various systems (Bronfenbrenner, 1989). Conducting this intervention within the ecological perspective implies that the clinician has a broad understanding of the child in his or her environment. Therefore, clinicians are encouraged to intervene on multiple levels, which might include meeting with parents, conducting teacher trainings, and engaging in case management to address the needs of the child's family. Within the ecological context, it is important to be aware of both risk and protective factors and to take a *strengths perspective* when examining the child within the ecological niche.

GTI for Children must be conducted with the participant's *cultural practices* in mind, especially death rituals and spiritual beliefs as well as coping strategies. It is also important to be aware of historical occurrences that may shape the beliefs and actions of the child and family. Furthermore, it is imperative that clinicians understand the language of the child participant.

The activities within GTI for Children focus on promoting *resilience and safety*, helping the child to tell the story in a more *restorative* manner, and helping the child connect or *reconnect* with supportive people (see Table 1.2 for a list of the activity themes). These activities are consistent with current research on childhood trauma as well as traumatic grief. For example, since social support has been found to be an important factor to buffer against complicated grief (Burke, Neimeyer & McDevitt-Murphy, 2010) and childhood posttraumatic stress disorder (Trickey et al., 2012), activities that include identifying and promoting social support are included. Similarly, a meta-analysis found that seeking social support, optimism and religious coping, and positive reappraisal coping contribute to posttraumatic growth (Prati & Pietrantoni, 2009). Activities consistent with promoting a more positive outlook and promoting resilience include: identifying supportive people; having the child seek a supportive person to share his or her book with (i.e., seeking social support); having the child identify things that he/she likes about his/her life; discussing a positive vision for his or her life (i.e., optimism); exploring spirituality by having the child write a prayer, poem, or song (i.e., religious coping); and helping the child to tell the story in a restorative manner which may lead to positive appraisal of the event(s) (i.e., positive reappraisal).

Some of the intervention strategies included in this manual that are based in CBT include the following: structured, time-limited intervention; relationship-based intervention; an educational component; making connections between thoughts, feelings, and behaviors; positive statements; relaxation; modeling and teaching; creating a coherent narrative; and imaginative exposure. In GTI for Children, children develop a story with a beginning, middle, and end about what happened. In an individual session with the clinician they also discuss the worst moment about what happened. Telling the story is approached from both a CBT perspective in that the telling and discussing exposes the child to the traumatic event in a safe, structured process, and from a narrative perspective where the meaning of the event and loss is explored. Cognitive behavioral therapy interventions that incorporate exposure are highly recommended for children after trauma (Foa et al., 2009).

Some of the strategies based on *narrative therapy* that are included in GTI for Children include: telling of the story with the focus on the meaning to the child; telling of stories with rich descriptions; exploring alternative stories and/or unique outcomes; retelling the story with a different outlook, recognizing that the problem did not occur within the child but rather is external; highlighting the child's strengths; using the child's language; and working collaboratively.

Making meaning of the loss is often a process undertaken over time by the bereaved. One might ask how someone can make meaning of a loss, especially if the loss occurred due to an unimaginable accident or a violent act. Interviews with 20 African American teens (ages 16 to 19) provide some insight into how children and youth may construct meaning after a traumatic loss and embrace elements of resilience after the murder of a friend. Early constructions of meaning relating to what happened entailed questioning why it happened; reviewing the events related to the death; assigning a rationale for the occurrence, including blame; and describing the associated emotions. Themes of metaphysical constructions were included as the youth struggled to make sense of the violent death. These constructions were sometimes rooted in religious beliefs and they helped to provide some understanding, e.g., "things happen for a reason," the person is "gone to a better place," and that in many ways they would "stay connected" to the deceased. Lastly, motivational constructions that helped promote growth and resilience were expressed, such as doing things or aspiring to improve themselves because they know the deceased person would want that for them, and having a deeper appreciation for life and friendships (Johnson, 2010).

Another way that children construct meaning related to loss is through continuing bonds to the deceased. Recalling memories, having ongoing dialogue with the deceased, believing in an external existence of the deceased, and maintaining an internal connection to the deceased are all ways children continue bonds with the deceased (Wood, Byram, Gosling & Stokes, 2012). These ongoing connections may also be developed based on spiritual beliefs and cultural practices. However, it may be that bereaved children who are experiencing trauma may not be able to maintain continuing bonds due to the trauma interrupting the grieving process.

While these theories guide the development and implementation of GTI for Children, there are three criteria that must be present when providing GTI for Children: (1) clinicians providing GTI for Children must enjoy working with children; (2) clinicians need to be able to easily develop rapport with children; and (3) the intervention must be provided in a caring compassionate manner.

STEPS FOR NARRATIVE ACTIVITIES – DDWW: DRAW, DISCUSS, WRITE, WITNESS

The drawing activities (see worksheets) follow the same format: Draw, Discuss, Write, and Witness (DDWW). Different children may feel more comfortable with different steps. Honor the child's natural inclination and spend more time using that method of expression, but encourage the child to use all steps (draw, discuss, write, and have others witness). In a group setting it is sometimes difficult to facilitate all of the steps, but with children who are working at different rates (i.e., some have finished the drawing while another has finished the writing) and with co-facilitation, the process of DDWW can work successfully in a group setting. Furthermore, the witnessing by the facilitators and group members can be very powerful for the child. These steps provide imaginative exposure and narrative detail and meaning.

1. **Draw**: Child uses drawing to portray imagery of the identified topic.
2. **Discuss**: Child and clinician discuss the drawing through a clinician-guided exploration including the child's thoughts and feelings about the topic.
3. **Write**: Child, with clinician assistance, writes the story about the topic. The written word provides the adult with whom the child shares the book at the end of the intervention insight into the child.
4. **Witness**: A caring "outside witness" person and/or group of people listen to the child's story (White & Epston, 1990) while paying attention to and empathetically responding to the child's emotions.

Table 1.2 *Overview of GTI for Children: Theory and Themes*

		Resilience	Restorative retelling	Reconnecting
		Cognitive behavioral and narrative practice methods		
		Draw, Discuss, Write, Witness		
Orientation	1	Orientation, anger management, relaxation		Begin reconnecting
	2	Orientation, education on grief and trauma, anger management, relaxation		Brief retelling – meaning
	3	Anger management, family changes/support, coping, spirituality, relaxation		Relationships (include to the deceased), meaning
Cohesion and mutual support	4	Feelings, education, questioning, prevention and safety, relaxation		
	5	Dreams, safety, relaxation		
	6	Relaxation	Retelling	
	Pull-out	Relaxation	Retelling, worst moment Correct distortions Address guilt Reinforce relaxation	Unique needs
	7	Coping, relaxation	Retelling, coherent narrative	Coping and supports
	8	Relaxation	Retelling Memories of loss(es)/deceased Meaning of loss(es)/relationship to deceased	Reconnecting and exploring meaning
Termination and separation	9	Relaxation	Retelling Memories Positive aspects and positive vision Discuss ending	Reconnecting, hope
	10	Relaxation	Celebrate progress, reconnecting	
		DEC: Developmentally appropriate, Ecological perspective, Culturally relevant		

GOALS AND OUTLINE OF GTI FOR CHILDREN

The main goals of GTI for Children are to provide psychoeducation about grief and traumatic stress, to provide a safe environment and structure for the child to express his or her thoughts and feelings about what happened and what the loss means to him or her, to decrease posttraumatic stress reactions to allow the normal grieving process to proceed, and to help build the child's coping capacity.

Thus, the main goals of GTI for Children are to help the child:

1. Learn more about grief and traumatic reactions.
2. Express his or her thoughts and feelings about what happened.
3. Decrease posttraumatic stress reactions.
4. Build coping capacity.

REFERENCES

Allen, B. & Johnson, J. C. (2012). Utilization and implementation of trauma-focused cognitive–behavioral therapy for the treatment of maltreated children. *Child Maltreatment, 17*(1), 80–85. doi:10.1177/1077559511418220

American Psychiatric Association (APA; 2013). *Diagnostic and statistical manual of mental disorders* (5th ed., DSM-5). Washington, DC: Author.

Baum, N. (2012). Trap of conflicting needs: Helping professionals in the wake of a shared traumatic reality. *Clinical Social Work Journal, 40*(1), 37–45. doi:10.1007/s10615-011-0347-0

Brewer, J. D. & Sparkes, A. C. (2011). Young people living with parental bereavement: Insights from an ethnographic study of a UK childhood bereavement service. *Social Science & Medicine, 72*(2), 283–290.

Bronfenbrenner, U. (1989). Ecological systems theory. *Annals of Child Development, 6,* 187–249.

Brown, A. C., Sandler, I. N., Tein, J., Liu, X. & Haine, R. A. (2007). Implications of parental suicide and violent death for promotion of resilience of parentally-bereaved children. *Death Studies, 31*(4), 301–335. doi:10.1080/07481180601187092

Brown, E. J., Amaya-Jackson, L., Cohen, J., Handel, S., Thiel de Bocanegra, H., Zatta, E., . . . Mannarino, A. (2008). Childhood traumatic grief: A multi-site empirical examination of the construct and its correlates. *Death Studies, 32*(10), 899–923. doi:10.1080/07481180802440209

Burke, L. A., Neimeyer, R. A. & McDevitt-Murphy, M. E. (2010). African American homicide bereavement: Aspects of social support that predict complicated grief, PTSD, and depression. *Omega, 61*(1), 1–24. doi:10.2190/OM.61.1.a

Cerel, J., Fristad, M. A., Verducci, J., Weller, R. A. & Weller, E. B. (2006). Childhood bereavement: Psychopathology in the 2 years postparental death. *Journal of the American Academy of Child and Adolescent Psychiatry, 45*(6), 681–690. doi:10.1097/01.chi.0000215327.58799.05

Cohen, J. A., Mannarino, A. P., Greenberg, T., Padlo, S. & Shipley, C. (2002). Childhood traumatic grief: Concepts and controversies. *Trauma Violence Abuse, 3*(4), 307–327. doi:10.1177/1524838002237332

Deblinger, E., Mannarino, A. P., Cohen, J. A., Runyon, M. K. & Steer, R. A. (2010). Trauma focused cognitive behavioral therapy for children: Impact of the trauma narrative and treatment length. *Depression and Anxiety, 28*(1), 67–75. doi:10.1002/da.20744

Dowdney, L. (2000). Annotation: Childhood bereavement following parental death. *Journal of Child Psychology and Psychiatry, 41*(7), 819–830. doi:10.1111/1469-7610.00670

Foa, E. D., Keane, T. M., Friedman, M. J. & Cohen, J. A. (2009). Treatment guidelines. In E. F. Foa, T. M. Keane, M. J. Frieman & J. A. Cohen (Eds.), *Effective treatments for PTSD: Practice guidelines from the International Society for Traumatic Stress Studies* (pp. 549–562). New York: Guilford Press.

Hagan, M. J., Luecken, L. J., Sandler, I. N. & Tein, J. (2010). Prospective effects of post-bereavement negative events on cortisol activity in parentally bereaved youth. *Developmental Psychobiology, 52*(4), 394–400. doi:10.1002/dev.20433

Herman, J. L. (1997). *Trauma and recovery*. New York: Basic Books.

Johnson, C. M. (2010). African American teen girls grieve the loss of friends to homicide: Meaning making and resilience. *Omega – Journal of Death and Dying, 61*(2), 121–143. doi:10.2190/OM.61.2.c

Kaplow, J. B., Layne, C. M., Pynoos, R. S., Cohen, J. A. & Lieberman, A. (2012). DSM-5 diagnostic criteria for bereavement-related disorders in children and adolescents: Developmental considerations. *Psychiatry: Interpersonal and Biological Processes, 75*(3), 243–266. doi:10.1521/psyc.2012.75.3.243

Kaplow, J. B., Shapiro, D. N., Wardecker, B. M., Howell, K. H., Abelson, J. L., Worthman, C. M. & Prossin, A. R. (2013). Psychological and environmental correlates of HPA axis functioning in parentally bereaved children: Preliminary findings. *Journal of Traumatic Stress, 26*(2), 233–240. doi:10.100/jts.21788

La Greca, A. M., Silverman, W. K., Vernberg, E. M. & Prinstein, M. J. (1996). Symptoms of posttraumatic stress in children after Hurricane Andrew: A prospective study. *Journal of Counseling and Clinical Psychology, 64*(4), 712–723. doi:10.1037/0022-006X.64.4.712

Layne, C. M., Saltzman, W. R., Poppleton, L., Burlingame, G. M., Pasalic, A., Durakovic, E., . . . Pynoos, R. S. (2009). Effectiveness of a school-based group psychotherapy program for war-exposed adolescents: A randomized controlled trial. *Journal of the American Academy for Child and Adolescent Psychiatry, 47*(9), 1048–1062. doi:10.1097/CHI.0b013e31817eecae

Luthar, S. S., Cicchetti, D. & Becker, B. (2000). The construct of resilience: A critical evaluation and guidelines for future work. *Child Development, 71*(3), 543–562. doi:10.1111/1467-8624.00164

March, S. M., Amaya-Jackson, L., Murray, M. C. & Schulte, A. (1998). Cognitive-behavioral psychotherapy for children and adolescents with posttraumatic stress disorder after a single-incident stressor. *Journal of the American Academy of Child and Adolescent Psychiatry, 37*(6), 585–593. doi:10.1097/00004583-199806000-00008

McClatchy, I. S., Vonk, M. E. & Palardy, G. (2009). The prevalence of childhood traumatic grief – a comparison of violent/sudden and expected loss. *Omega – Journal of Death and Dying, 59*(4), 305–323. doi:10.2190/OM.59.4.b

Melhem, N. M., Moritz, G., Walker, M., Shear, M. K. & Brent, D. (2007). Phenomenology and correlates of complicated grief in children and adolescents. *Journal of the American Academy of Child and Adolescent Psychiatry, 46*(4), 493–499. doi:10.1097/chi.0b013e31803062a9

Melhem, M. D., Porta, G., Shamseddeen, W., Payne, M. W. & Brent, D. A. (2012). Grief in children and adolescents bereaved by sudden parental death. *Archives of General Psychiatry, 68*(9), 911–919. doi:10.1001/archgenpsychiatry.2011.101

Nader, K. & Salloum, A. (2011). Complicated grief reactions in children and adolescents. *Journal of Child and Adolescent Trauma, 4*(3), 233–257. doi:10.1080/19361521.2011.599358

Nixon, R. D. V., Sterk, J. & Pearce, A. (2012). A randomized trial of cognitive behaviour therapy and cognitive therapy for children with posttraumatic stress disorder following single-incident trauma. *Journal of Abnormal Child Psychology, 40*(3), 327–337. doi:10.1007/s10802-011-9566-7

Northen, H. & Kurland, R. (2001). *Social work with groups* (3rd ed.). New York: Columbia University Press.

Perry, B. D. (2009). Examining child maltreatment through a neurodevelopmental lens: Clinical applications of the neurosequential model of therapeutics. *Journal of Loss and Trauma: International Perspectives on Stress and Coping, 14*(4), 240–255. doi:10.1080/15325020903004350

Prati, G. & Pietrantoni, L. (2009). Optimism, social support, and coping strategies as factors contributing to posttraumatic growth: A meta-analysis. *Journal of Loss and Trauma: International Perspectives on Stress and Coping, 14*(5), 364–388. doi:10.1080/15325020902724271

Raphael, B. & Martinek, N. (1997). Assessing traumatic bereavement and posttraumatic stress disorder. In J. P. Wilson & T. M. Keane (Eds.), *Assessing psychological trauma and PTSD* (pp. 373–395). New York: Guilford Press.

Rynearson, R. (2001). *Retelling violent death*. Philadelphia: Brunner-Routledge.

Salloum, A. (2008). Group therapy for children experiencing grief and trauma due to homicide and violence: A pilot study. *Research on Social Work Practice, 18*(3), 198–211. doi:10.1177/1049731507307808

Salloum, A., Avery, L. & McClain, R. P. (2001). Group psychotherapy for adolescent survivors of homicide victims: A pilot study. *Journal of the American Academy of Child and Adolescent Psychiatry, 40*(11), 1261–1267. doi:10.1097/00004583-200111000-00005

Salloum, A., Carter, P., Burch, B. Garfinkel, A. & Overstreet, S. (2011). Impact of exposure to community violence, Hurricane Katrina, and Hurricane Gustav on posttraumatic stress and depressive symptoms among school age children. *Anxiety, Stress and Coping, 24*(1), 27–42. doi:10.1080/10615801003703193

Salloum, A., Garfield, L., Irwin, A., Anderson, A. & Francois, A. (2009). Grief and trauma group therapy with children after Hurricane Katrina. *Social Work with Groups, 32*(1–2), 67–79. doi:10.1080/01609510802290958.

Salloum, A. & Overstreet, S. (2008). Evaluation of individual and group grief and trauma interventions for children post disaster. *Journal of Clinical Child and Adolescent Psychology, 37*(3), 495–507. doi:10.1080/15374410802148194

Salloum, A. & Overstreet, S. (2012). Grief and trauma intervention for children after disaster: Exploring coping skills versus trauma narration. *Behaviour Research and Therapy, 50*(3), 169–179. doi:10.1016/j.brat.2012.01.001

Shaw, J. A., Applegate, B., Tanner, S., Perez, D., Rothe, E., Campo-Bowen, A. E. & Lahey, B. L. (1995). Psychological effects of Hurricane Andrew on an elementary school population. *Journal of the American Academy of Child and Adolescent Psychiatry, 34*(9), 1185–1192. doi:10.1097/00004583-199509000-00016

Silverman, P. R. & Worden, W. (1992). Children's reactions in the early months after the death of a parent. *American Journal of Orthopsychiatry, 62*(1), 93–104. doi:10.1037/h0079304

Spuij, M., Reitz, E., Prinzie, P., Stikkelbroek, Y., de Roos, C. & Boelen, P. A. (2012). Distinctiveness of symptoms of prolonged grief, depression, and post-traumatic stress in bereaved children and adolescents. *European Child Adolescent Psychiatry, 21*(12), 673–679. doi:10.1007/s00787-012-0307-4

Stoppelbein, L. & Greening, L. (2000). Posttraumatic stress symptoms in parentally bereaved children and adolescents. *Journal of the American Academy of Child and Adolescent Psychiatry, 39*(9), 1112–1119. doi:10.1097/00004583-200009000-00010

Stroebe, M. & Schut, H. (1999). The dual process model of coping with bereavement: Rationale and description. *Death Studies, 23*(3), 197–224. doi:10.1080/074811899201046

Tosone, C., Nuttman-Shwartz, O. & Stephens, T. (2012). Shared trauma: When the professional is personal. *Clinical Social Work Journal, 40*(2), 231–239. doi:10.1007/s10615-012-0395-0

Trickey, D., Siddaway, A. P., Meiser-Stedman, R., Serpell, L. & Field, A. P. (2012). A meta-analysis of risk factors for post-traumatic stress disorder in children and adolescents. *Clinical Psychology Review, 32*(2), 122–138. doi:10.1016/j.cpr.2011.12.001

Walsh, F. (2003). Family resilience: A framework for clinical practice. *Family Process, 42*(1), 1–18. doi:10.1111/j.1545-5300.2003.00001.x

Walsh, W. A., Dawson, J. & Mattingly, M. J. (2012). How are we measuring resilience following childhood maltreatment? Is the research adequate and consistent? What is the impact on research, practice, and policy? *Trauma, Violence and Abuse, 11*(1), 27–41. doi:10.1177/1524838009358892

White, M. (2007). *Maps of narrative practice*. New York: W. W. Norton.

White, M. & Epston, D. (1990). Narrative means to therapeutic ends. New York: W. W. Norton & Company.

Wood, L., Byram, V., Gosling, A. S. & Stokes, J. (2012). Continuing bonds after suicide bereavement in childhood. *Death Studies, 36*(10), 873–898. doi:10.1080/07481187.2011.584025

Worden, W. J. (1996). *Children and grief: When a parent dies*. New York: Guilford Press.

Worden, W. J. & Silverman, P. R. (1996). Parental death and the adjustment of school-age children. *Omega, 33*(2), 91–102. doi:10.2190/P77L-F6F6-5W06-NHBX

Chapter 2

Getting Ready to Implement GTI for Children

This chapter provides a brief overview of creating a supportive environment for the successful implementation of GTI for Children as well as a discussion of how to use this manual. This chapter also addresses common questions that are asked when someone considers implementing GTI for Children, such as who should participate and what needs to be considered when first starting GTI for Children.

ENVIRONMENTAL SUPPORT

A major barrier to implementing evidence-based practices is the gap between researchers, treatment developers, and clinicians because clinical research and clinical practice often occur separately (Teachman et al., 2012). GTI for Children was developed in community settings where both research and practice knowledge were integrated during the development of the model. This process led to an empirically-informed intervention that can be easily applied in a practical manner, and a treatment manual that is straightforward and allows for flexibility while still maintaining fidelity to treatment. To be proactive in light of implementation barriers, the following list of statements is meant to be used as a quick guide for promoting a supportive environmental context for implementation of GTI for Children.

Further exploration and discussion are needed prior to the implementation of GTI for Children if the answer to any of these statements is false.

Please answer True or False to the following statements:

Attitudes:

1. I believe that outcomes similar to those obtained in the treatment trials can be obtained in my practice with GTI for Children.
2. I believe a strong therapeutic relationship can be developed while using a structured treatment.
3. I can use my creativity when implementing GTI for Children and still maintain treatment fidelity.
4. If GTI for Children is implemented within an agency, the key agency staff should be knowledgeable about the structure of GTI for Children and the empirical support for the intervention.
5. All stakeholders involved (therapist, supervisors, agency administrators, funders) believe that GTI for Children should be provided and that it will be beneficial for the children (i.e., there is "buy-in" on all levels).
6. I have the resources (i.e., copies, therapeutic materials, supervision) and time needed to deliver the intervention, and if GTI for Children is being provided within the agency, the agency will provide the facilitators with the time needed to implement GTI for Children.

Clinical Preparation:

7. I have current knowledge about the impact of trauma on children.
8. I am able to tolerate the intense emotional expression and listen to stories of bereaved and traumatized children.
9. I enjoy working with children.
10. I have a good understanding of cognitive behavioral therapy and narrative therapy.
11. I recognize the potential impact of working with children experiencing grief and trauma and actively engage in my own self-care plan.
12. I have read *Grief and Trauma in Children: An Evidence-Based Treatment Manual* in its entirety.

Logistics:

13. I have addressed the critical logistics (i.e., consents, available time for implementation, consistent space, and materials) for implementing GTI for Children.
14. Standardized assessment measures can be administered before and after the intervention.
15. I have access to clinical supervision from someone who is knowledgeable about clinical practice with children experiencing childhood bereavement and trauma.

HOW TO USE THIS MANUAL

Prior to implementation of GTI for Children it is recommended that the clinician read the entire manual so that he or she has a broad overview of the intervention. Once the intervention begins, clinicians are encouraged to engage in the following activities:

Before each session, read in full that *session* section. In some of the sessions a **"Note"** and/ or **"Tip"** paragraph may be included. Notes provide additional insight into other considerations and tips provide suggestions for making the sessions proceed more smoothly.

Review the *agenda* before each session and use it to guide the session. If there are two facilitators decide who will lead and co-lead each activity.

Copy the *worksheets* that will be needed for that session. The worksheets have the session number on the bottom so that it is easy to find what worksheets go with the particular session number, and having the worksheets together in the Appendix makes copying them easy. You may photocopy any page that has this icon.

After each session, complete the *adherence checklist*. Make note of any themes that occurred that were not part of the agenda, and decide if and how these topics need to be addressed.

After each group session, make time to review how it went (see *post-session review*). Address the following:

- Structure
- Content
- Dynamics
- Individual progress
- Co-leading process
- Own reactions
- Next session.

Attend weekly clinical supervision to discuss each session, as needed.

TIPS FOR FACILITATING THE SESSIONS

1. Always begin and end in the same manner. Begin and end each meeting with a relaxation technique (it is helpful to use deep breathing because it reinforces the importance of using this technique and it does not take a lot of time).
2. An hour and 15 minutes is recommended for each session, but this is often not possible, especially in a school setting. Therefore, try to have at least an hour available for each session. This extra time allows for the beginnings and endings and sufficient time to complete the activity for that session.
3. Inform the child(ren) about what will be covered in the session.
4. Let the child(ren) know that this is not an English or art class. Therefore, they do not have to worry about writing neatly or spelling correctly, and the drawings can be completed quickly – even by using stick figures if a child wishes.
5. Let the child choose the worksheet he or she wants to work on during each session. Many of the sessions allow the child to pick one of the worksheets. This choice gives the control

to the child and allows the child to guide the clinician rather than vice versa. For example, in session 2 there are three worksheets with the themes of trauma, grief, and loss. The child can choose which one is more salient for him or her at that time or which one he or she is able to tolerate at that time.

6. Always let the child(ren) know how much time is allotted for each activity and inform them when the time is running out (i.e., "Only two more minutes" and "Okay now only one more minute").

7. When working with children in a group, it may be more important to move to the next activity even if one child is not completely finished. Reassure children that they may go back to finish a particular worksheet at another time. This way the group can move on to the next topic, and children can return to various uncompleted worksheets at their own pace.

8. If a child finishes one of the activities and is waiting on the others, have him or her spend some time decorating his or her book by coloring in the titles of the worksheets. These were purposefully created in block letters so that children can color these in when waiting on the group to proceed.

9. We do not recommend allowing the children to play when waiting on other children because some children may rush to complete the grief and trauma activity so that they can play.

CRITERIA FOR PARTICIPATION

The following inclusion and exclusion criteria were used in the clinical treatment trials on GTI for Children. There may be other reasons for excluding a child that are not mentioned here. For example, children who had comorbid conditions were not excluded from the trials. However, if the child's presenting concerns are not related to grief and trauma, another type of treatment may be warranted prior to participating in GTI for Children. For example, if the child has untreated attention deficit hyperactivity disorder (ADHD) that is causing severe impairment and would make it difficult for the child to participate in GTI for Children, appropriate treatment for ADHD is needed first.

GTI for Children may be provided individually or with a group of children since both modalities have been demonstrated to be effective. Clinicians have also used GTI for Children with sibling groups and in family therapy. However, if siblings are participating in a group with other children, clinical judgment will need to be used about keeping them in the same group, as participating together may prevent them from getting their individual needs met. GTI for Children was developed and tested with children ages 7 to 12. Clinicians have used GTI for Children with 6-year-olds as well as with young teenagers. However, it is critical that the intervention be delivered in a way that matches the child's developmental age. For teenagers who enjoy drawing, GTI for Children may be a good fit. However, we recommend using a model explicitly developed for teenagers such as *Group work with adolescents after violent death: A manual for practitioners* (Salloum, 2004).

Inclusions:

1. Age 7 to 12 years and/or grades 2nd through 6th.
2. Experiencing at least moderate level of traumatic stress due to loss, death, violence, or

disaster. GTI for Children was tested with children with multiple traumas, but it may also be used for children with single-incident traumas.

3. Grieving (must be at least one month post-loss/death). The grief does not have to be only related to a death and not every child in the group may be grieving. It is best to have homogeneous groups, but since that is not always feasible it is not a necessity.

4. If GTI for Children is provided with a group of children, the child must be clinically appropriate for group participation (i.e., able to complete the assessment, seems to be able to focus on the tasks at hand, clinical impressions indicate that the child is appropriate for group participation).

5. The child wants to participate and, of course, parental permission has been granted.

Exclusions:

1. Suicidal. Use a standardized depression screening instrument to screen for suicidality. Assessment will need to occur to distinguish between statements about wanting to be with the deceased versus wanting to die or kill themselves. It is important that a trained mental health clinician assess the severity of the suicidal ideation. If the child is suicidal, seek immediate appropriate intervention. Inform the parent and have the child evaluated by an appropriate mental health professional. The child must be stabilized before participating in this intervention. This may include individual therapy, family therapy, medication, and appropriate follow-up.

2. Cognitive impairments. If the child is not able to understand the assessment questions, participation is not warranted.

ABUSE, NEGLECT, AND DOMESTIC VIOLENCE

Since GTI for Children is often implemented in schools, school officials are sometimes hesitant to allow for screening of abuse, neglect, and domestic violence. The research studies to date on GTI for Children did not include a screening with the child for abuse, neglect, or domestic violence. However, the parent assessments during these studies did include screening questions about children's exposure to these types of traumatic events. In these studies, parents indicated that many of the children had experienced these types of traumas in addition to the other identified traumas, such as witnessing community violence, having a loved one die, or experiencing stress due to a disaster.

If a child discloses abuse, neglect, or domestic violence during the intervention, the appropriate authorities need to be contacted and additional services need to be provided as appropriate. The child's safety is the number one priority. It may be appropriate to remain in GTI for Children while also receiving individual or family counseling.

CRITICAL LOGISTICS

Most private practice clinicians and agencies already have most of the critical logistics that are needed to deliver mental health care in place. Therefore, in this section a brief review of important logistics for delivering GTI for Children is presented as a reminder.

Written agreement between provider and host setting. If GTI for Children is provided in an off-site location (i.e., not in the private practitioner or agency office), it is important that there is a memorandum of agreement between the provider and site personnel where the intervention will be provided. In this agreement, the experience and background of the clinicians should be provided along with what will be provided and needed from the host setting (see example of Memorandum of Understanding).

Consents. A written consent form that is traditionally used for providing psychotherapy should be obtained for a child to participate in GTI for Children. This form should include a brief statement indicating that the parent and child will be asked to complete an assessment to see if GTI for Children may be an appropriate intervention for the child. If the assessment information indicates that the child meets the criteria to participate in GTI for Children, the intervention will be provided, and if not, other options and resources will be discussed with the parent/guardian. In some cases, it may be decided that consent forms will be sent to all parents/guardians from certain groups (such as all third and fourth graders) and then assessments will occur with children whose parents consented, or consent forms may only be sent to parents/guardians of children who have been identified by staff such as counselors, teachers, social workers, or psychologists who are aware that the child is experiencing grief and trauma.

On-site coordinator/contact. If GTI for Children is being provided off-site (i.e., not in provider's office or agency) it is important to have an on-site coordinator who can assist with setting up the group, such as securing private, consistent space; establishing the schedule of when the intervention will occur; identifying children for participation; and obtaining consent forms.

Consistent, private, adequate space. The amount of space needed is based on the number of children who will be receiving GTI for Children. For example, if GTI for Children is provided individually, a small room will be needed; if GTI for Children is provided in a group, a room that holds a table seating about 8 to 10 people would be ideal. In order to create a safe therapeutic environment, it is important that the space is private (i.e., not in the lunch room or teacher lounge where people may be coming in and out of the room) and available for every session.

Engaged clinicians with time for processing and facilitators meetings. GTI for Children sessions typically last an hour, although they may be provided in an hour and a half if time permits. In the clinical trials on GTI for Children, the sessions lasted one hour or sometimes less depending on how long it took to get the children from the classrooms. Facilitators need to plan time before and after each session to prepare for the session and to conduct a post-session review. In addition, when GTI for Children is conducted in a school or a community-based setting, we recommend that a follow-up facilitators meeting is planned the week following the final session. Having a planned time to meet once the group has ended allows the facilitators to review the progress of each child and to discuss any further recommendations as to what may be needed. Also, if a child was not present during the final meeting, the facilitators can meet with the child during this time.

Resources for materials. The following materials will be needed: standardized instruments for assessment and evaluation (this cost will vary depending on the measures used), copies of the worksheets in the back of the manual, crayons and markers, books that are suggested throughout the manual or other therapeutic books, materials for making coping collages or other coping reminder activities, certificates for completing the intervention, and snacks (especially if provided after school) and other food items for celebrating intervention completion during the final session.

Date:

To: [name organization such as the school where GTI for Children will be provided]

From: [name provider(s)]

RE: MEMORANDUM OF UNDERSTANDING BETWEEN [PROVIDER] AND [COMMUNITY ORGANIZATION]

Grief and Trauma Intervention (GTI) for Children is an evidence-based grief and trauma intervention for children ages 7 to 12 who are experiencing grief and trauma due to violence, death, and disasters. GTI for Children is listed in the National Registry of Evidence-Based Programs and Practices which is sponsored by the United States Department of Health and Human Services Substance Abuse and Mental Health Services Administration (SAMHSA).

GTI for Children has been tested with children experiencing posttraumatic stress due to witnessing or being a direct victim of violence (often multiple types of violence), death of a loved one (including homicide), and disasters (specifically, Hurricane Katrina). The intervention employs cognitive behavioral and narrative therapy strategies to effectively and significantly reduce symptoms of posttraumatic stress, depression, and traumatic grief in children. GTI for Children has been implemented in various community-based settings, including schools, afterschool programs, and community centers, and may be provided individually or in a group setting.

As part of this memorandum of agreement, [name provider] will provide GTI for Children at [name organization and give address where intervention will be held]. The providers of GTI for Children will be [name providers and give statement about background of providers]. Children who qualify for GTI for Children will be provided services at [add cost information] if they are between the ages of 7 to 12, experiencing at least a moderate level of posttraumatic stress, and experiencing a significant loss. The goals of GTI for Children are for each child to (1) learn more about grief and traumatic reactions, (2) express his or her thoughts and feelings about what happened, (3) decrease posttraumatic stress reactions, and (4) build coping capacity. Parents must provide written consent for their child to participate in the intervention as well as provide brief background information about the child.

As part of this agreement, [name community organization] agrees to:

1. Allow [name provider] to provide GTI for Children to identified children at [name location] between the dates of [name dates].
2. [Name provider] will provide a private, adequate-sized room that can be used consistently for implementing GTI for Children.
3. [Name provider] will identify an on-site coordinator who may assist with referring children to GTI for Children, obtaining consent forms and other organizational needs for implementing GTI for Children.

Signature of Provider _____ Date _____

Signature of Recipient _____ Date _____

REFERENCES

Salloum, A. (2004). *Group work with adolescents after violent death: A manual for practitioners.* Philadelphia, PA: Brunner-Routledge.

Teachman, B. A., Drabick, D. A. G., Hershenberg, R., Vivian, D., Wolfe, B. E. & Goldfried, M. R. (2012). Bridging the gap between clinical research and clinical practice: Introduction to the special section. *Psychotherapy: Theory, Research and Practice, 49*(2), 97–100. doi:10.1037/a0027346

Chapter 3

Practitioner Support

This chapter is placed at the beginning of this manual rather than at the end as a way to remind clinicians providing GTI for Children to practice self-care. This chapter provides information on burnout, secondary traumatic stress, and vicarious traumatization which are processes and conditions that occur due to work-related stress, especially when working with traumatized populations. The positive benefits of working with survivors of trauma are also discussed as well as ways to buffer against the negative effects of working with trauma survivors. The GTI for Children model provides clinicians with pre- and post-session tools to help them prepare to work with children, prepare for the next meeting, and monitor their own reactions to working with children experiencing grief and trauma.

WORKER STRESS AND SELF-CARE

Burnout, secondary traumatic stress, and vicarious traumatization have overlapping negative consequences. Burnout is the result of work demands and may result in physical, mental and emotional exhaustion; depersonalization; and decreased feelings of personal accomplishment (Kahill, 1988). Secondary traumatic stress (also known as compassion fatigue) is the result of consistently being exposed to traumatic stories and content from others resulting in behavioral and emotional consequences (Figley, 1995; Nelson-Gardell & Harris, 2003). Vicarious traumatization, which is also a result of distress due to working with people who have experienced trauma, is when one experiences cognitive changes in beliefs related to trust, safety, power, independence, esteem, and intimacy (McCann & Pearlman, 1990). Whether one is experiencing burnout, secondary traumatic stress, or vicarious traumatization, these conditions can cause symptoms and impairment such as depression, difficulty sleeping, loss of intimacy with friends and family (Canfield, 2005), and possibly PTSD. In fact, in the DSM-5, there is recognition that one may develop PTSD from "repeated or extreme exposure to adverse details of the traumatic event(s)" (APA, 2013, p. 271).

Professionals who provide therapy to children who have experienced trauma need to be aware of potential effects on their well-being. In a meta-analysis of studies on the impact of vicarious trauma on professionals working with survivors of sexual violence and child sexual abuse, all of the studies reported some degree of negative psychological disruption. This review examined several key variables associated with vicarious traumatization, and while there has been some support found for these risk factors, the findings are still mixed, most likely due to methodological limitation. However, several of the studies found that higher levels of exposure and lower levels of experience working with trauma survivors were key factors associated with high levels of vicarious trauma (Chouliara, Hutchinson & Karatzia, 2009). Factors that contribute to work-related stress may occur on the organizational level, personal level, client level, or a combination of these levels.

Some studies also suggest that professionals experience positive benefits from working with survivors such as increased spiritual and existential well-being (Chouliara et al., 2009), increased awareness of one's own family members' needs, better control of anger, and development of communication and assertiveness skills (Ben-Porat & Itzhaky, 2009). In fact, researchers are exploring the concept of vicarious posttraumatic growth among those who treat people who are traumatized (e.g., Barrington & Shakespeare-Finch, 2012; Lambert & Lawson, 2012). For example, in a qualitative sample of 17 staff (clinicians and managers) who work with survivors of torture and trauma, the workers discussed positive changes in how they viewed life (e.g., less judgmental; sense of gratitude; more open; more aware; changed values and priorities; appreciative of love, freedom, and safety; increased religiosity and spirituality), their selves (e.g., seeing themselves as strong and confident), and interpersonal relationships (e.g., connecting with those who have shared values and beliefs, advocating for trauma victims within interpersonal relationships) (Barrington & Shakespeare-Finch, 2012). Recent research suggests that therapist posttraumatic growth (e.g., growth in relationships with others, sense of self, and philosophy of life) may serve as a buffer against the impact of secondary traumatic stress which can lessen the impact of negative changes such as depression, anxiety, and decreased personal meaning and satisfaction with life (Samios, Rodzik & Abel, 2012).

Self-reflection, reflection with a supportive supervisor, and formal assessment are ways to monitor and identify when one may be experiencing work-related distress. Newell and MacNeil (2010) suggest that agencies and organizations should regularly administer measures to determine and monitor work-related stress. Validated instruments include the Maslach Burnout Inventory (Schaufeli, Bakker, Hoogduin, Schaap & Kladler, 2001), the Secondary Traumatic Stress Scale (Bride, Robinson, Yegidis & Figley, 2004), and the Professional Quality of Life (Stamm, 2010). These measures may also be used for self-assessment and could be discussed with a supportive supervisor.

Some of these validated work-related stress measures as well as other self-care measures can be found at www.proqol.org and www.socialwork.buffalo.edu/resources/self-care-starter-kit.html.

The National Child Traumatic Stress Network has developed a fact sheet for child-service professionals on secondary traumatic stress that provides helpful educational information (see www.nctsn.org/sites/default/files/assets/pdfs/secondary_traumatic_tress.pdf).

Practicing within a trauma-informed care environment may be another way to guard against burnout, secondary traumatic stress, and vicarious traumatization, and increase positive benefits of working with children experiencing grief and trauma. Specialized trauma-focused training where the worker increases skills and effective practice and cultivates peer support may buffer against the negative effects of trauma work (Sprang, Clark & Whitt-Woosley, 2007).

TRAUMA-INFORMED CARE

Trauma-informed care is a framework to provide care in an environment in which systems and services are supportive to trauma survivors. Those working from a trauma-informed care perspective understand how trauma impacts people. Providers work collaboratively with survivors in a respectful, empowering manner that provides hope for recovery. Providers also understand the profound impact of trauma and how trauma exposure is connected to symptoms of trauma. Within the trauma-informed perspective, trauma-specific evidence-based treatments are offered to survivors (National Center for Trauma-Informed Care, nd). The National Child Traumatic Stress Network has an initiative to promote trauma-informed care among child welfare workers. They have set forth nine essential elements for trauma-informed child welfare practices: (1) maximize the child's sense of safety; (2) assist children in reducing overwhelming emotions; (3) help children make new meaning of their trauma history; (4) address the impact of trauma and subsequent changes in the child's behaviors, development, and relationships; (5) coordinate services with other agencies; (6) utilize comprehensive assessment of a child's trauma experience and the impact on the child's development and behavior to guide services; (7) support and promote positive and stable relationships in the life of the child; (8) provide support and guidance to the child's family and caregivers; and (9) manage professional and personal stress (Child Welfare Committee, National Child Traumatic Stress Network, 2008). Creating and maintaining a trauma-informed care practice takes considerable training and "buy-in" at all levels of management (administrators, supervisors, front-line staff) (Kramer, Sigel, Conners-Brown, Savary & Tempel, 2013).

The GTI for Children model, which is considered a trauma-specific intervention, contains elements of the trauma-informed child welfare practices when it is utilized within a trauma-informed model. For example:

1. Helping children to develop a *sense of safety* is specifically addressed in session 5, and other coping techniques for developing a sense of safety are addressed in other sessions.
2. The first four sessions focus on helping the child to *manage overwhelming emotions*; session 4 includes an activity about feelings and the pull-out session inquires more about guilt, which is often an intense, difficult-to-handle emotion.
3. GTI for Children uses the DDWW method to help children *make new meaning of their trauma history*.
4. Through reduction of symptoms and an increase in the use of coping strategies, the *impact of trauma and subsequent changes in the child's behaviors, development, and relationships will be addressed* in some areas.
5. GTI for Children is provided within an ecological perspective which encourages advocacy for the child and family and *coordination with other services* that may be of help to the child and family.
6. Standardized *assessments* of the child's symptoms (i.e., PTSD, depression, traumatic grief), behaviors (internalizing and externalizing behaviors), and other areas such as peer relations, academic performance, social support, and other salient domains are recommended for guiding treatment and monitoring treatment progress.
7. Identifying and *promoting positive supportive people* in the child's life is congruent with two of the phases of the intervention – resilience and reconnecting. The child is encouraged

in the first session to identify supportive people who he/she can share his/her thoughts and feelings with about what happened. Also, when addressing coping skills, children are encouraged to get coping assistance (i.e., sharing of thoughts and feelings, doing things with caring others, etc.) from supportive people. Lastly, the intervention ends with the child sharing, with a caring adult, the book he/she developed as part of the intervention.

8. At least one meeting with the parent/caregiver is recommended, where the clinician can *provide support to the caregiver* by educating him/her about grief and trauma, and provide any needed referrals to services that may help the family and/or caregiver.

9. The GTI for Children book includes a chapter on self-care as well as pre- and post-session tools to support and encourage clinicians to practice self-care and *manage stress*.

Table 3.1 provides some general signs and symptoms to identify possible work-related distress, and Table 3.2 provides suggestions for ways to mitigate the negative effects of working with trauma survivors.

Table 3.1 *Signs and Symptoms of Work-Related Distress*

Burnout	Emotional exhaustion
	Detached (cynical, negative, pessimistic and detached from others including co-workers and clients)
	Feelings of inadequacies to help others
Secondary stress	Intrusive thoughts, memories or nightmares related to client trauma
	Difficulty sleeping
	Fatigue
	Difficulty concentrating
	Avoidance of clients, work related to clients and client situation
	Hypervigilant toward client trauma reminders
	Intense feelings of guilt or anger
Vicarious traumatization	Changes in sense of self and esteem such as feelings of helplessness or incapable of change
	Changes in views of safety such as "the world is not safe" and "I am not safe"
	Changes in trust and intimacy such as "I cannot trust anyone anymore" or "I no longer feel close to the ones I love"
	Weakening in spiritual beliefs

Note: There are other signs and symptoms of work-related stress, and there may be overlap between the different conditions listed above (Canfield, 2005; Newell & MacNeil, 2010).

Table 3.2 *Possible Ways to Mitigate Negative Effects of Working with Trauma Survivors*

Personal strategies:

    Recognize the need to prioritize self-care and one's personal life

    Create time every day for self-care

    Maintain a balance between professional and personal life

    Have an optimistic perspective

    Develop coping strategies to manage and tolerate intense affect

    Hold a belief of altruism

    Have a sense of a higher purpose in life

    Exercise regularly and maintain physical health (fitness, mindfulness, nutrition, sleep)

    Engage in enjoyable recreational activities

    Engage in self-expression (talking, writing, drawing, painting, gardening, and so on)

    Seek therapy when needed

Professional strategies:

    Maintain clear boundaries

    Utilize affective distancing

    Engage with a professional support system and create a supportive team environment

    Have and utilize a supportive available supervisor

    Recognize personal positive outcomes of working with trauma survivors (finding meaning and satisfaction)

    Celebrate personal and professional achievements

    Continue to increase clinical skills to assist trauma survivors with positive outcomes (use of evidence-based practices)

    Work collaboratively with clients

Professional/organizational strategies:

    Enhance awareness and education in relation to the effect of job distress, especially with trauma survivors

    Legitimize one's experience of work-related distress

    Allocate resources for ways to build-in preventative strategies (i.e., skilled and available supervisor, mental health days off, flexible times for work schedule, training to build expertise, workshops on coping with job stress)

    Reduce caseload of working with trauma survivors

Note: There may be other ways to mitigate negative effects of working with trauma survivors but this list provides many of the ways cited in the literature (e.g., Ben-Porat & Itzhaky, 2009; Canfield, 2005; Barrington & Shakespeare-Finch, 2012; Figley, 2002; Harrison & Westwood, 2009; Lambert & Lawson, 2012).

PRE AND POST CLINICIAN MEETINGS

Working with traumatized and bereaved children can be very rewarding, but it can also be very taxing. It is important for clinicians to prepare themselves before meeting with the children. Also, it is just as important to participate in a systematic review *after* meeting with the children. The following outlines provide a pre-meeting review that is to be implemented before every session, and a post-meeting review that is to be implemented after every session.

PRE-SESSION REVIEW

1. Clinician preparation

The first person to prepare is yourself (the clinician). It is important that you take some time and center yourself before facilitating a GTI for Children session. We suggest that you practice deep breathing or positive self-talk before beginning and also try to clear your mind of other work-related and personal matters so that you can focus on the child/children. Also, if you are using GTI for Children in a group format, it is important that you check your patience level. Working with many traumatized children at one time takes a lot of patience and focus. After preparing yourself, use the following rating scales related to calmness, patience, and focus to assess your current level. A rating of 6 to 7 is ideal.

How calm do I feel?

	1	2	3	4	5	6	7
Not calm at all			Somewhat calm				Very calm

What is my level of patience?

	1	2	3	4	5	6	7
Not feeling patient			Feel somewhat patient			Feel I can be very patient	

How focused is my mind on facilitating this session?

	1	2	3	4	5	6	7
Not focused			Somewhat focused				Very focused

If GTI for Children is being delivered in a group format, we suggest that the co-workers share their responses to these questions with each other before starting each group and discuss how they can support each other during the session.

2. Session preparation

Read the goals and notes for each session in this book before conducting the session. Do you have all of the supplies that are needed? Also, look at your post-session review notes from the prior session to prepare for the upcoming session.

POST-SESSION REVIEW

Structure:
Was the setting conducive to treatment (i.e., private, comfortable temperature, adequate space, appropriate seating arrangements)?
How effective was the therapy structure (beginning, middle, and end) and do any changes need to be made?

Content:
What were the major themes of the session?
Were any comments/topics raised but not adequately addressed? If so, will this topic(s) be addressed next session or in another session and if so, how?
What was the notable clinical content for each child participant?

Group dynamics:
How would you describe the overall group dynamics?
Are there cliques or subgroups being formed; if so, do these help or hinder the group process?
Is any member taking on a role (such as the "jokester" or "clown") that is preventing him or her from reaching his or her own goals?
Are group norms helping the group to remain focused on the goals?
Is there a sense of group cohesion? Has the group developed enough for cohesion to be present? If cohesion is not being developed and the middle of the treatment (sessions 4–5) is approaching, how can more cohesion be encouraged?

Individual progress:
Review each group member and ask – has he or she participated actively and meaningfully in the essential topics and activities?
On a scale of 1 to 10 (with 1 being no progress on goal attainment and 10 being goals met), where is each child on this scale?

Co-leading:
How did the co-leading process work? Did the co-leaders support each other or was there confusion about who was leading which activity?
What could be done differently to improve the co-leaders' collaboration?
What changes are suggested before the next session?

Facilitators' reactions:
What feelings came up for the facilitators during the group?
Were there any upsetting thoughts that came up during the group?
What are the overall reactions to the group session?
What stress management plans will you practice today and this week?

Next session:
Will the next session follow the group format or does it need to be slightly modified?

Source: Adapted from A. Salloum (2004) *Group work with adolescents after violent death.* New York: Brunner-Routledge.

REFERENCES

American Psychiatric Association (APA; 2013). *Diagnostic and statistical manual of mental disorders* (5th ed., DSM-5). Washington, DC: Author.

Barrington, A. J. & Shakespeare-Finch, J. (2012). Working with refugee survivors of torture and trauma: An opportunity for vicarious post-traumatic growth. *Counselling Psychology Quarterly, 26*(1), 89–105. doi:10.1 080/09515070.2012.727553

Ben-Porat, A. & Itzhaky, H. (2009). Implications of treating family violence for the therapist: Secondary traumatization, vicarious traumatization, and growth. *Journal of Family Violence, 24*(7), 507–515. doi:10.1007/s10896-009-9249-0

Bride, B. E., Robinson, M. M., Yegidis, B. & Figley, C. R. (2004). Development and validation of the secondary traumatic stress scale. *Research on Social Work Practice, 14*(1), 27–35. doi:10.1177/1049731503254106

Canfield, J. (2005). Secondary traumatization, burnout, and vicarious traumatization. *Smith College Studies in Social Work, 75*(2), 81–101. doi:10.1300/J497v75n02_06

Child Welfare Committee, National Child Traumatic Stress Network (2008). *Child welfare trauma training toolkit: Comprehensive guide* (2nd ed.). Los Angeles, CA & Durham, NC: National Center for Child Traumatic Stress.

Chouliara, Z., Hutchinson, C. & Karatzia, T. (2009). Vicarious traumatization in practitioners who work with adult survivors of sexual violence and child sexual abuse: Literature review and directions for future research. *Counseling and Psychotherapy Research, 9*(1), 47–56. doi:10.1080/1473314082656479

Figley, C. R. (1995). *Compassion fatigue.* New York: Brunner/Mazel.

Figley, C. R. (2002). Compassion fatigue: Psychotherapists' chronic lack of self care. *Journal of Clinical Psychology, 58*, 1433–1441.

Harrison, R. L. & Westwood, M. J. (2009). Preventing vicarious traumatization of mental health therapists: Identifying protective practices. *Psychotherapy: Theory, Research, Practice, Training, 46*(2), 203–219. doi:10.1037/a0016081

Kahill, S. (1988). Interventions for burnout in the helping professions: A review of the empirical evidence. *Canadian Journal of Counseling Review, 22*(3), 310–342.

Kramer, T. L., Sigel, B. A., Conners-Burrow, N. A., Savary, P. E. & Tempel, A. (2013). A statewide introduction of trauma-informed care in a child welfare system. *Children and Youth Services Review, 35*(1), 19–24.

Lambert, S. F. & Lawson, G. (2012). Resilience of professional counselors following hurricanes Katrina and Rita. *Journal of Counseling and Development, 91*(3), 261–268. doi:10.1002/j.1556-6676.2013.00094.x

McCann, L. & Pearlman, L. A. (1990). Vicarious traumatization: A framework for understanding the psychological effects of working with victims. *Journal of Traumatic Stress, 3*(1), 131–149.

National Center for Trauma-Informed Care (nd). *Welcome to the National Center for Trauma-Informed Care. United States, Substance Abuse & Mental Health Services Administration.* http://beta.samhsa.gov/nctic (accessed October 7, 2014).

Nelson-Gardell, D. & Harris, D. (2003). Childhood abuse history, secondary traumatic stress, and child welfare workers. *Child Welfare, 82*(1), 5–26.

Newell, J. M. & MacNeil, G. A. (2010). Professional burnout, vicarious trauma, secondary traumatic stress, and compassion fatigue: A review of theoretical terms, risk factors, and preventive methods for clinicians and researchers. *Best Practices in Mental Health, 6*(2), 57–68.

Salloum, A. (2004). *Group work with adolescents after violent death: A manual for practitioners.* Philadelphia, PA: Brunner-Routledge.

Samios, C., Rodzik, A. K. & Abel, L. M. (2012). Secondary traumatic stress and adjustment in therapists who work with sexual violence survivors: The moderating role of posttraumatic growth. *British Journal of Guidance and Counseling, 40*(4), 341–356. doi:10.1080/03069885.2012.691463

Schaufeli, W. B., Bakker, A. B., Hoogduin, D., Schaap, C. & Kladler, A. (2001). On the clinical validity of the Maslach burnout inventory and the burnout measure. *Psychology and Health, 16*(5), 565–582. doi:10.1080/08870440108405527

Sprang, G., Clark, J. J. & Whitt-Woosley, A. (2007). Compassion fatigue, compassion satisfaction, and burnout: Factors impacting a professional's quality of life. *Journal of Loss and Trauma: International Perspectives on Stress and Coping, 12*(3), 259–280. doi:10.1080/15325020701238093

Stamm, B. H. (2010). The Concise ProQOL Manual (2nd ed.). Pocatello, ID: ProQOL.org

Chapter 4

Screening and Evaluating

This chapter provides information about the use of assessment tools for screening for participation, monitoring, and evaluation. An interview protocol for the first assessment is provided as a guide. Information about group composition and co-leaders is provided for GTI for Children when utilized with a group of children. To help practitioners use the assessment information to guide the treatment, a clinical chart is presented. The clinical chart may be copied and completed by the practitioner as a way to have accessible assessment information to guide treatment.

ASSESSMENT TOOLS AND EVALUATION

Using standardized assessment instruments before and after GTI for Children is an important way to understand the impact of trauma and loss, screen for the appropriateness of GTI for Children, guide treatment, and track progress. Some practitioners may think that these evaluation measures are burdensome to the child and family. However, when measures are administered in a caring and informative manner, many children and parents find the evaluation session to be very helpful. The evaluation process can actually be used to provide education about childhood grief and trauma.

There are many different types of measures of childhood posttraumatic stress and depression and, recently, measures of childhood traumatic or complicated grief have been developed. Clinicians need to make sure that the measures used are reliable and valid. Particular attention needs to be paid to making sure that the child understands the questions being asked. Usually permission has to be obtained to use standardized measures. Five categories of measures are recommended: (1) a broad-based assessment; (2) trauma and grief-focused exposure assessments; (3) trauma and grief-focused mental health assessments; (4) strengths, resiliency-based (protective factors) measures; and (5) goals attainment and satisfaction. The broad-based assessment is usually completed by the parent/caregiver, whereas the other more specific measures can be completed by the child.

The standardized measures that are typically used with GTI for Children include the following:

1. Exposure to death: Experiences Survey of Having Someone Close Die (Salloum, 2010). This assessment tool is included in this manual and it is used to assess for loss(es) due to death and details about the death. It is clinician-administered with the child.

2. Exposure to community violence: Survey of Children's Exposure to Community Violence (adapted from Richters and Martinez, 1993). The six-item measure assesses for exposure to community violence. A copy is included in the manual. This measure can be completed by the child or clinician-administered.

3. Posttraumatic stress: The UCLA Posttraumatic Stress Disorder Index (UCLA-PTSD-Index; Pynoos, Rodriquez, Stienberg, Stuber & Frederick, 1998). The measure assesses for exposure to different types of potentially traumatic events and for posttraumatic stress symptoms. It is also used to screen children for moderate levels of posttraumatic stress, the main criterion for participation. This measure is completed by the child. Or, you may use the Child PTSD Symptom Scale (CPSS; Foa, Johnson, Feeny & Treadwell, 2001). The CPSS scale may be obtained at www.performwell.org

4. Depression: The Mood and Feelings Questionnaire-Child Version (MFQ-C; Angold & Costello, 1987). This measure assesses for symptoms of depression, and there are five items that may be used to screen for suicidal ideation. This measure is administered to the child.

5. Traumatic grief: Check the National Child Traumatic Stress Network website for new postings of childhood grief measures.

6. Treatment goals and satisfaction: Grief and Trauma Intervention Review of Goals. This instrument is included in the manual in the Appendix section. It is to be administered after children participate in GTI for Children and it provides a way to receive feedback about goal attainment.

7. Disaster exposure: If GTI for Children is being used after a disaster, the National Center for Childhood Traumatic Stress has brief screening tools to elicit the child's experiences.

Broad-based measure: The broad-based measure that has been used with GTI for Children is the Child Behavior Checklist (Achenbach & Rescorla, 2001) which is completed by the parent. This measure provides an assessment of the child's competencies, peer relations, academic performance, and total behavior problems including internalizing and externalizing behaviors. For more information about this measure see www.aseba.org

Another broad-based measure that may be useful is the Strengths and Difficulties Questionnaire. This measure assesses emotional symptoms, conduct problems, hyperactivity/inattention, peer relationship problems, and pro-social behaviors. There is also a follow-up section to be used after treatment that inquires about the impact of treatment. For more information see www.sdqinfo.com

These broad-based measures have teacher versions that can be very helpful for assessing the child and evaluating treatment.

Young children cannot sit for a long period of time to answer questions; therefore, make sure the measures used are brief and the assessment process is not too long. Typically, the assessment process takes about 30 to 45 minutes with each child. We recommend that each child is seen individually for the assessments, and that all items are read aloud to the child. It is helpful to give the child the response format for each measure so that he/she remembers the response options, and to read them each time a question is asked. If a child becomes fidgety and starts to drift, allow the child to take a short break, perhaps by walking to get a drink of water. Also, if the child becomes distressed during the assessment, pause the assessment, teach the child how to breathe deeply, and have him/her practice until his/her distress is reduced. Depending on the child's level of distress, the assessment may or may not be completed. If the child cannot complete the assessment, then group intervention is not indicated; we would consider individual or family counseling. The First Meeting with Child: Interview Format for Individual Screening with Child provides a protocol guide for conducting the assessment.

It is important to double check that all information has been completed on all surveys before ending the assessment.

For more information about obtaining these and other measures, such as coping or social support, see the following:

1. The National Child Traumatic Stress Network, "Measures" section: www.nctsn.org
2. The California Evidence-Based Clearinghouse for Child Welfare also has a list of screening and assessment tools. See www.cebc4cw.org/assessment-tools
3. The National Center for PTSD has information on measures for childhood PTSD. See www.ptsd.va.gov/professional/pages/assessments/child-trauma-ptsd.asp

When requesting a copy of the measures, inquire about any updates to the measure based on the DSM-5 diagnosis.

EVALUATOR

Minimum qualifications to administer many psychological measures, especially self-report measures, require a master's degree in a related mental health field. Other measures may not require that the administrator have a master's degree, but that training on administration of the selected measures is obtained. It is very important that the evaluator is familiar with the selected evaluation instruments and has undergone some type of training about administering the measures.

We recommend that the evaluator, who will conduct pre-, post-, and, if possible, follow-up assessments, is a different person than the group facilitators or clinician who provide GTI for Children. Consider asking another clinician who is not providing GTI for Children to the selected children to serve as an evaluator. This way these two roles (i.e., treating clinician and evaluator) are kept separate and this will help to minimize response bias. After the pre-intervention assessment is completed and the child meets criteria to receive GTI for Children, it is helpful for the group facilitator or clinician to review the assessment information to learn more about the child. The group facilitators or clinicians should also review post-intervention evaluator results about each child so that progress can be shared with parents and appropriate recommendations can be made.

NOTE

While the "Format for Individual Screening" is used to guide the initial meeting, it may also be used at the end of the intervention to evaluate the intervention. Evaluation measures include measures of posttraumatic stress, depression and childhood traumatic grief, global questions about how distressed the child has been in the past month, open-ended questions about coping, and the goal review form (see Appendix). Clinicians may also want to include assessments with parents and teachers.

FIRST MEETING WITH CHILD: INDIVIDUAL SCREENING WITH CHILD

Goals:

1. Explain purpose and process of intervention to the child.
2. Make sure criteria for participation are met.
3. Learn about child's perception of "what happened" (how life-threatening/scary) and meaning of the loss(es).
4. Assess multiple losses and traumas and level of distress.
5. Conduct pre-test measures.
6. Briefly assess and highlight child's strengths and coping.
7. Inform child of intervention schedule.

Before the child participates in GTI for Children it is important to meet with the child individually to make sure that the child meets the criteria for participation and to learn more about the child. This first meeting can also help the child to feel more comfortable once the sessions begin. This first meeting allows for two crucial parts of the intervention to take place: assessment and evaluation. The assessment will provide the clinician with a better understanding of the child and what he or she may need, and the evaluation will help the clinician know if the goals for the intervention have been met. The "First Meeting with Child: Format for Individual Screening with Child" form provides an outline for the assessment process. It is recommended that this form be completed initially and again at the end of the intervention so that an overall evaluation of effectiveness can be made.

FIRST MEETING WITH CHILD: FORMAT FOR INDIVIDUAL SCREENING WITH CHILD

Name of child: _____

School: _____

Date: _____

Evaluator: _____

Format: _____

- Inform the child of what the two of you will be doing.
- Try and help the child feel more comfortable.
- Explain the purpose and process of intervention to the child.
- Assess for losses and potentially traumatic events.
- Administer the exposure to trauma and loss questionnaires. Administer standardized PTSD, depression, traumatic or complicated grief instruments as well as other selected instruments such as coping or social support.
- While briefly discussing traumatic incident(s), try to learn about the child's perception of "what happened" (how life-threatening/scary) and meaning of the loss(es). When asking a lot of questions about exposure, it is often helpful to use a simple response format (such as yes and no), although this may not capture the frequency of the event.

After reviewing the experiences list, ask "Are there other things that have happened in your life that made you feel really upset or scared?"

_____

_____

_____

If more than one loss or trauma, ask:
  "Of all the things we have talked about [may name some of them]":
  Which one bothers you the most?

_____

Which one makes you feel the saddest?

_____

Which one is the hardest for you to talk about?

_____

How distressed (upset, mad, stressed, sad, or irritable) have you been in the past month as a result of [name the trauma or loss(es)]? Circle one:

None   A little   Some   Much of the time   Most of the time

Let the child know that you will be asking a lot of questions about how he/she has been and is thinking and feeling about [name trauma, loss] during the past two weeks, and that many of these questions are because other children have felt the same way after something terrible happens. The timeframe of two weeks was chosen because, while PTSD measures usually ask children about symptoms in the past month and depression measures usually ask about symptoms in the past two weeks, it is too difficult to ask children to think about different timeframes and to think back to longer periods of time. Therefore, we suggest keeping the timeframe the same for all measures.

1. Administer measure of posttraumatic stress.
2. Administer measure of depression.
3. If applicable, administer measure of traumatic grief or complicated grief.
4. If another measure was selected, such as coping or social support, administer it.

Briefly assess and highlight child's strengths and coping.

1. What has helped you cope (or deal) with [name traumatic incidents] so far? (i.e., what helps you feel better?)

_____

_____

_____

2. What kinds of things do you do for fun?

_____

_____

_____

3. Who do you have that you can talk with about your thoughts and feelings about what has happened?

_____

_____

_____

4. How has this been for you talking about these things that happened? <u>Note if the child was able to talk easily or if the child became visibly upset.</u>

_____

_____

_____

Make sure criteria for participation are met:

Age 7 to 12 in elementary school (2nd through 6th grade).   Yes or No

Grieving (must be at least one month post-loss/death).   Yes or No

Experiencing at least moderate level of traumatic stress due to loss/death/   Yes or No
violence/disaster.

Not suicidal. Look at answers on depression screening. If the child is having
suicidal thoughts seek immediate appropriate intervention. Inform the parent
and have the child evaluated by an appropriate mental health professional.
The child is to be stabilized before participating in this intervention. This may
include individual therapy, family therapy, medication, and appropriate
follow-up.   Yes or No

If group treatment is being provided, the child is clinically appropriate for group
participation (i.e., able to complete the assessment, seems to be able to focus on
the tasks at hand, clinical impressions indicate that the child is appropriate
for group participation).   Yes or No

The child wants to participate.   Yes or No

If criteria are met, inform the child of the schedule (start day, time, etc.). Once the schedule has been confirmed, make sure the child and parent have a copy of the schedule of when and where GTI for Children will occur. If GTI for Children is being provided at school or with a community group, make sure the coordinator and others such as teachers, receptionist, and principal all have a copy of the schedule.

NOTE

If the child has a difficult time remaining focused during the intervention, build in a break time when the child can get a drink of water or take a stretching break.

If the child becomes too overwhelmed during the assessment and is not utilizing or does not have a lot of resources (e.g., adult support, can calm self and self-soothe, participation in recreational activities, able to talk about intense feelings and/or positive memories, etc.), this intervention may not be appropriate for this child at this time.

Also, if a child expresses that he or she does not want to participate, this too might be an indication that this type of intervention is not right for the child at this time.

INSTRUCTIONS FOR EXPERIENCES SURVEY OF HAVING SOMEONE CLOSE DIE

This semi-structured interview is to determine: (1) if the child had someone close die, (2) the cause of death, (3) when the death occurred, (4) the child's relationship to the deceased, and (5) whether the child witnessed the death. The evaluator is to read aloud the questions below and complete the chart on the second page based on the child's answers. Any additional details shared by the child are to be recorded in the notes section. Explain that for the first question, the child is to only answer "yes" or "no." If the child answers "no," stop the interview. If the child answers "yes," explain that you would like to ask only a few more questions to learn a little bit more about what happened.

1. I have had a family member or someone close to me die. Circle yes or no on the chart.

    1.a. If no, stop the interview.

    1.b. If yes, ask "Have you had <u>one</u> family member or person close to you die or <u>more than one</u> family member or person close to you die?" If a child states more than one person, the questions will need to be asked about each person who died. Fill out the chart based on all deaths. A separate form may be used for each death or one form for all deaths.

    1.c. So that you can use the person's name during the interview, ask "What is the person's name who died?" If more than one person died, "What are the people's names who have died?"

2. How did [insert name(s)] die? If the child does not answer quickly, ask was it due to (list the different causes of death listed on the chart)?
3. When did the person(s) die?

Try to obtain the exact date. Many times young children do not remember the day, month, or year. Therefore, asking questions about the timeframe is helpful. For example, "Was it this school year, this summer, or last school year? Fall or spring?" If it was during the school year, you may ask the timeframe in reference to holidays. For example, "Did ___ die before Halloween (or before Thanksgiving and so on)?" If it was during the summer, you may ask "Was it closer to when you got out of school or closer to when school began?" If the child states a month, you may ask "Do you remember if it was the beginning of the month or the end of the month?" and then record either the first or the last day of the month. If only a month is stated, record the first day of the month and the year.

4. How was [either insert name(s) or state *this person*] related to you?

Write the name of the person who died *and* the <u>relationship</u> to the child.

Use the following relationship categories:

Parent: Mother or Father	Sibling: Brother or Sister	Aunt or Uncle
Stepmother or Stepfather	Grandmother or Grandfather	Cousin
Friend	Neighbor	Other: state relationship

5. Now, I am going to ask a few more questions about what you saw.

Use the yes or no questions first as a way to minimize the amount of detail that the child shares at this point in an effort to not overwhelm the child. Clinically, a broad definition of "witnessed" is used, defined as: the child actually witnessed the dying of the person; the child was in very close proximity during or *immediately* after the dying; or the child witnessed any element related to the dying event such as the dead body, the body bag, blood, heard the person yell or make noises, bullet holes, etc. Based on the child's responses, the evaluator determines if "witnessed" is endorsed or not. Also, any details shared should be written in the notes section. Ask 5.a and 5.b.

5.a. **"Did you see the person dying?"** Ask yes or no.

5.b. **"Were you there when they died or right after they died?"** Ask yes or no.

5.c. If yes to 5.a or 5.b. ask, **"Did you see anything that made you feel upset or scared?"** Ask yes or no.

5.d. If yes to 5.c, ask, **"Can you tell me in a few words what you saw?"**

EXPERIENCES SURVEY OF HAVING SOMEONE CLOSE DIE (SALLOUM, 2010)

Complete the following chart, based on the five questions stated on the instructions.

1. I have had a family member or **someone close** to me die. Circle: Yes or No

2. CAUSE	3. YEAR/MONTH	4. WHO/RELATIONSHIP	5. WITNESSED
Accident	_____	_____	yes no

If yes, check type of accident:

❑ Motor Vehicle   ❑ Fire   ❑ Poisoning   ❑ Fall   ❑ Drowning   ❑ Firearms
❑ Medical/Surgery complications

Other: _____

Suicide (person killed themselves)	_____	_____	yes no
Homicide (person killed by someone else)	_____	_____	yes no
Heart attack	_____	_____	yes no
Cancer	_____	_____	yes no
Stroke	_____	_____	yes no
Disease	_____	_____	yes no

If yes, state the type of disease: _____

Natural causes (like old age)	_____	_____	yes no
Other	_____	_____	yes no

Provide additional details shared by the child about the death and/or the person who died (if more than one death, make sure to clearly record which notes are for which death).

_____

_____

_____

_____

VIOLENCE EXPOSURE SURVEY (ADAPTED FROM RICHTERS AND MARTINEZ, 1993)

Answer the statements based on things you have seen in <u>real life</u>.
Please circle the number of times you have seen the following.

How often:	0 Times	1 Time	2 Times	3 Times	Many Times
I have seen somebody get stabbed	0	1	2	3	4
I have seen somebody get shot	0	1	2	3	4
I have seen a dead body outside or in my home	0	1	2	3	4
I have seen someone get hurt really badly	0	1	2	3	4
I have seen a crime scene after someone died	0	1	2	3	4
I have seen somebody dying	0	1	2	3	4

Notes:

_____

_____

_____

_____

_____

_____

_____

_____

_____

_____

GROUP COMPOSITION AND CO-LEADERS

When meeting with groups of children, it is recommended that the group composition consist of children who have experienced similar types of losses. For example, it may be that everyone in the group has lost their home due to a disaster or that everyone in the group has had someone close to them die. It would be preferable that even the type of death be similar, such as death due to the disaster. Homogeneous groups are important because common concerns and subtle issues pertaining to the presenting problem can be addressed. Also, if there are major differences in the types of losses, children may compare and minimize other children's losses. However, if it is not possible to have homogeneous groups, it is acceptable to have groups where children have experienced different types of losses and traumatic events. The facilitators will need to link common experiences of loss and traumatic stress.

Generally, children in a group should be no more than two years apart, and group intervention should not occur until at least one month post death or loss.

In practice, these recommendations may not be possible. Therefore, clinicians will need to have strategies to help all children feel safe and see commonalities. For example, clinicians may explain that "everyone in the group has had something scary or sad happen", or "everyone in the group has had something scary or sad happen that is difficult to talk about. In this group we are going to make it a safe place so that when you are ready, you can share what has happened."

It is best to keep the group size to six children. However, if most of the children in the group are older, the group size can be as large as eight. Two co-leaders are recommended as younger children often need individual time with an adult facilitator. One co-leader may be a bachelor, master, or doctoral level student intern or experienced volunteer if two mental health professionals are not available.

USE OF THE CLINICAL CHART

After a child has been accepted to participate in GTI for Children, it is important that the clinician always keep in the forefront what has happened to the child and the child's strengths since both (trauma and loss, and strengths) will be addressed. It is recommended that the clinician complete the Clinical Chart form in order to quickly learn about all group members' experiences and as a constant reminder of each child's trauma, loss(es), and strengths.

From the assessment information, write down the child's strengths, what he or she identified as the "index" trauma or primary trauma that the assessment was conducted on, what bothers the child the most or is the most difficult to talk about, and what makes the child feel the saddest. Sometimes these are all the same and sometimes they are different events. Also, make sure you have a parent's name and contact information on the chart in case the parent needs to be contacted.

CLINICAL CHART

If the child had someone close die, make sure you note, who (by name), relationship to child, when, and how.

Child's name	Parental contact	Bothers most	Saddest	Hardest to talk about	Strengths/ activities for fun	Comments

REFERENCES

Achenbach, T. M. & Rescorla, L. A. (2001). *Manual for the ASEBA School-Age Forms & Profiles.* Burlington, VT: University of Vermont, Research Center for Children, Youth & Families.

Angold, A. & Costello, E. J. (1987). Mood and Feelings Questionnaire. Developmental Epidemiology Program, Duke University. devepi.mc.duke.edu/mfq.html (accessed October 7, 2014).

Foa, E. B., Johnson, K. M., Feeny, N. C. & Treadwell, K. R. (2001). The Child PTSD Symptom Scale: A preliminary examination of its psychometric properties. *Journal of Clinical Child Psychology, 30*(3), 376–384.

Pynoos, R. S., Rodriquez, N., Stienberg, A., Stuber, M. & Frederick, C. (1998). *The UCLA Posttraumatic Stress Reaction Index for DSM IV.* Los Angeles: UCLA Trauma Psychiatric Program.

Richters, J. E. & Martinez, P. (1993). The NIMH Community Violence Project: I. Children as victims of and witnesses to violence. *Psychiatry: Interpersonal and Biological Processes, 56,* 7–21.

Salloum, A. (2010). Experiences survey of having someone close die. Unpublished assessment.

Chapter 5

Parents and Other Important Adults

This chapter provides information to be addressed with the parent or caregiver during the parent meeting. A brief personal information form is provided so that facilitators can learn more about the child and family. In addition, two handouts are provided to help parents understand common grief and trauma reactions and learn ways that they can help their child. If GTI for Children is being conducted within a larger child-serving organization, such as within a school or afterschool program, it is important for the teachers and/or staff to be educated about how to support a grieving child. A brief outline is provided for facilitators to use when talking with teachers and/or staff. Also, if the teachers and/or staff have been through the same traumatic event as the child, such as a disaster or school shooting, a teacher/staff "check-in" protocol is provided.

PARENTS/CAREGIVERS

When meeting with the parent, the clinician will want to understand what the parent has told the child about the manner of the death or related information. It is also important to understand if there is information that the parent has avoided telling the child and what their concerns may be if the child finds out this information. The clinician will want to work with the parent to foster open communication between the parent and the child. It is important that parents use age-appropriate language and avoid euphemisms and metaphors to describe the death as these can be confusing to the child. If the child believes that the deceased person "went to sleep" or has "gone to another place" the child may be afraid to go to sleep or may not understand the permanency of the death. Children need to be told in a brief, simple, matter-of-fact manner the cause of the death. Children do not need to be told associated details but they need to have enough information so that they can begin to have a story about what happened, eliminate misunderstandings, and not be left to fill in the details or fantasize about what occurred. For children who seem fixated on the way the person died, it is often helpful for the parent to let the child know that the person who died is no longer experiencing pain so that the child does not continue to worry about such concerns. It is also helpful to let parents know that some children may grieve intermittently and that as the child develops, the grieving process may continue. The child may continue to share his or her thoughts and feelings about the loss and may find new ways to express grief (Mitchell et al., 2006).

PARENT/CAREGIVER MEETING AGENDA

When providing GTI for Children, at least one meeting with the parent/caregiver needs to occur. Additional meetings may be held as needed. Ideally, the clinician should meet with the parent/caregiver before the child starts participating in GTI for Children. However, when providing GTI for Children in community-based settings with many children, it may not be possible to meet with all of the parents/caregivers before the intervention begins. In these cases, the meeting with the parent/caregiver needs to occur at least before the fourth session.

The goals and tasks to be accomplished when meeting with the parent/caregiver are as follows:

1. Review consent and explain purpose of the intervention to make sure the parent/caregiver understands the purpose of the intervention.
2. Gather assessment information pertaining to the traumatic experience and loss and other information such as if the child has learning challenges. See sample "Brief Personal Information Form."
3. Conduct a general assessment of the needs of the caregiver.
4. Provide education/normalization about grief and trauma with school-age children, and ways that parents can help children (explain deep breathing exercise and that the child will be working on using different strategies to calm him or herself down). See sample handouts, "Reactions of School Age Children After Traumatic Events and Loss(es)" and "What You Can Do To Help Your Child."
5. Make referrals as needed to help caregivers with their own trauma and grief. Leave a community resource list with the caregiver.
6. Stress importance of attending emotionally to the child and encourage open communication/sharing of what the child is talking about in the intervention. (Note: make sure the caregiver has specifically told the child the reason for being in the intervention and that the caregiver has clearly informed the child that it is okay to talk and share his/her thoughts and feelings.)
7. Give the parent a copy of the schedule of the GTI for Children sessions. See "Schedule."

TIP

Whenever possible provide children and families with direct support, for instance, help them to get food, clothing, shelter, etc. If needed, case management services are encouraged as a way to help the family in this time of stress.

NOTE

Parental contact is key. Once the parent signs the consent (if it was sent home from school) it may take a while to schedule a face-to-face meeting, but keep trying. Also, letters are a good way of keeping parents informed. Consider sending letters at the beginning of the intervention to let the parents know the intervention has begun and how they may contact the clinicians, during the middle of the intervention to let them know their child's progress, and at the end to provide any needed recommendations. If at any time the parent wants to meet, or if the clinician thinks a parent or family meeting is needed, these should be scheduled.

BRIEF PERSONAL INFORMATION FORM

Parent/Guardian (who is completing this form):

Name: _____ Relationship to child: _____

Name of child: _____

Current address: _____ Apt. # _____

City: _____ State: _____ Zip code: _____

Home phone: _____ Work phone: _____ Cell phone: _____

Email: _____

Current relationship status:
❑ Single ❑ Married ❑ Partnered ❑ Divorced ❑ Separated ❑ Widowed

Occupation: _____

Yearly household income (check one):
❑ $0 to $9,999   ❑ $35,000 to $49,999
❑ $10,000 to $24,999   ❑ $50,000 and above
❑ $25,000 to $34,999

Date of birth of child participant: _____
Race/ethnicity of child participant: _____

Gender of child participant: circle Male or Female

Family: Please include all persons living in the household with the child participant including yourself.

Name	Relationship to child	Age and birth date (M/D/YY)

Health and Medical:

Has your child ever been in counseling/therapy before or seen a psychiatrist? Yes or No

If yes, when: _____ and for what: _____

Is your child currently seeing a professional for mental health? Yes or No

If yes, who are they seeing: _____ Phone: _____

Is your child currently on any type of medication? Yes or No

If yes, what type of medication and for what: _____

_____

List any past or present physical/medical problems:

_____

Education History:

Did your child attend this school last year? Yes or No

Special education: Yes or No

Average behavior grade: _____

How many times has your child been suspended this year? _____

Describe any behavior problems, if any: _____

_____

Other Information:

Has your child ever witnessed domestic violence (pushing, screaming, hitting, etc.)? Yes or No

If yes, explain: _____

Has your child ever witnessed a shooting or stabbing? Yes or No

If yes, explain: _____

Has your child ever experienced any type of abuse? Yes or No

If yes, explain: _____

Has your child had someone close die? Yes or No

If yes, who (relationship to child):_____ When: _____

Cause of death: _____ Witnessed death: Yes or No

If yes, explain: _____

_____

Has your child experienced any other type of traumatic event? Yes or No

If yes, explain:

_____

_____

What concerns you most now about your child?

_____

_____

REACTIONS OF SCHOOL AGE CHILDREN AFTER TRAUMATIC EVENTS AND LOSS(ES)

- Increase in physical complaints such as stomachaches, headaches.
- Change in school performance (drop in academic performance, behavioral problems at school).
- Fear and worry about their safety and the safety of family and friends and/or that the bad thing will happen again.
- Angry outbursts, tantrums, or being more irritable.
- Sleep problems (difficulty falling/staying asleep, nightmares).
- More clingy than usual (younger children).
- Decrease in concentration and paying attention.
- Talking repeatedly about what happened, acting out the event in play.
- Increased sensitivity to loud noises (more jumpy) or reminders about the traumatic event (such as for hurricanes, children may be "on alert" and nervous when they hear heavy rain, wind, thunder).
- Regressive behaviors (bedwetting and tantrums).
- Lack of interest in usually fun activities.
- Avoiding any reminders (including talking) about what happened.

Seek Help, Don't Wait

After a disaster or traumatic event it is common for children to experience some of the reactions listed above. However, if these reactions continue for more than a month or if some of these reactions are causing problems in the child's social, emotional, behavioral, or academic life, professional mental health help may be needed. In fact, some children after disaster, death, violence, abuse, or other types of traumatic situations may develop what is called posttraumatic stress disorder (PTSD). Children with posttraumatic stress may have nightmares; distressing daydreams; become upset upon reminders about the trauma; try to avoid reminders; be withdrawn, unhappy, or more aggressive; and have difficulty sleeping and concentrating. These types of symptoms can have severe negative effects on the child's life. PTSD usually does not just go away with time, but there are treatments that can help children. Please talk with a mental health professional to learn more.

SUPPORTING YOUR CHILD

Show your child love every day. During stressful times your child may need your help more than usual. Here are some ways you can help.

What You Can Do to Help Your Child

- Establish consistent, nurturing bedtime routines.
- Find a consistent time to talk with your child(ren) (for example, at bedtime, mealtimes, in the car).
- Encourage your child(ren) to ask questions. Let him/her know it is okay to ask questions and to share his/her worries.
- Reassure your child(ren) frequently that you are safe and will keep him/her safe.
- Talk on his/her level. Don't lecture him/her or get too complicated.
- Reassure your child(ren) that things are getting better. If a disaster has occurred, tell him/her about the recovery being made.
- Limit media exposure. Protect your child from graphic images and adult conversations about what happened (including TV, newspaper, internet, radio).
- Take care of your own and your child's physical health. Make sure both of you are getting enough rest, exercise, and healthy food.
- Pay attention to your child(ren)'s play. It may give you a better understanding of his/her questions and concerns.
- Maintain family routines if at all possible (meals, bedtimes, play).
- Remember to praise your child, give hugs, and tell him/her that you love him/her!

Family Activities (try a few)

- Create a list of "things I can do to feel better" with your child.
- Read a children's book with your child related to rescue, recovery, or hope.
- Plan and have a family game night.
- Try a relaxation technique: find a comfortable position and practice deep breathing with your child(ren). Slowly count to seven breathing in and slowly count to seven breathing out. Repeat. Talk about how it feels to be relaxed.
- Plan a weekly activity with your child(ren) that can help you all take breaks from the stress (ride bikes, make dinner together, read a book together, play a game).
- Develop a Safety Plan with your child(ren). Let the child(ren) help in preparing the plan.

GTI FOR CHILDREN GROUP SCHEDULE

We _____ will be facilitating
a group at _____. The group will be time-limited
with a total of ten group sessions. We will also meet with you one time individually during the course
of this time. Group sessions will be held once a week in _____ room. Each session
lasts _____.

THE SCHEDULE FOR THE GROUP IS AS FOLLOWS:

SESSION	DATE	DAY	TIME
1			
2			
3			
4			
5			
6			
7			
8			
9			
10			

If you have any questions, or if we can be of assistance to you or your family, please call us at
_____.

If this intervention is held at school it may be important to rotate the days and times so that children
do not miss the same class. Children need to know when they will be attending the sessions. Make sure
that parents, teachers/staff, school officials, and children all have a copy of the schedule.

GTI FOR CHILDREN INDIVIDUAL SCHEDULE

My name is _____ and I will be working with you in a program called Grief and Trauma Intervention (GTI) for Children. We will be meeting a total of ten times. Sessions will be held once a week in _____ room. Each session lasts _____, but one session may last a bit longer, or we may schedule to have one additional session.

THE SCHEDULE FOR THE SESSIONS IS AS FOLLOWS:

SESSION	DATE	DAY	TIME
1			
2			
3			
4			
5			
6			
7			
8			
9			
10			

If you have any questions, or if I can be of assistance to you or your family, please call me at
_____.

If this intervention is held at school it may be important to rotate the days and times so that children do not miss the same class. Children need to know when they will be attending the sessions. Make sure that parents, teachers/staff, school officials, and children all have a copy of the schedule.

TEACHERS AND STAFF EDUCATION AND "CHECK-INS"

It is important that teachers and staff working with children have an understanding of childhood grief and traumatic stress and are skilled in working empathetically with children. If this intervention is conducted within a school, an afterschool program, or any child setting (such as a church group or camp), it is recommended that the clinicians provide the teachers/staff with an educational training and be available to them throughout the intervention to offer support and assistance. The training should include common *reactions* of children experiencing grief and trauma, ways for teachers/staff to *respond*, encouragement of *relaxation* and self-care among teachers/staff, and available *resources* in the school and community.

Sometimes teachers/staff may not want to participate in a training or support group due to not having enough time or because they are experiencing their own grief and traumatic stress. While a community approach (training, support group) is recommended, it may not be feasible. However, it is important that teachers are calm and not experiencing stress that negatively affects their teaching and interactions with children. If the teachers/staff have also been affected by the same trauma/loss as the children, one approach may be for the clinicians to conduct individual check-ins. The protocol for individual check-ins is as follows.

Purpose. In an effort to provide support for teachers/staff who have been affected by the same traumatic event(s) as the children in GTI for Children, teacher/staff "check-ins" are conducted individually with each teacher. The purposes of the individual meetings are as follows:

1. To provide educational information about common reactions to what has happened (death, disaster, violence, etc.) and the aftermath.
2. To raise awareness of coping strategies.
3. To learn about what teachers/staff may need to support them during this time of recovery so that they may be more available to meet the needs of the children.
4. To provide a list of community resources, including information about mental health services.

Protocol. Although the main topics of education, coping, resources, and teacher needs should be briefly discussed with all teachers, these check-ins are also a time to provide a listening, caring ear to teachers who may not have had a chance to talk and who may just need to have someone listen to their "story" and concerns. Therefore, first and foremost, empathic listening is essential. Teachers should be notified by the principal that counselors will be meeting with them once individually during a specific week during their planning period.

The individual teacher/staff check-in protocol is a way to establish personal relations with teachers to provide them support and hear what they need. However, it is recommended that if time allows, educational workshops and/or teacher support groups are conducted to provide additional, ongoing support.

The following is an outline for conducting individual teacher/staff check-ins, but it may also be used as a guide for conducting educational presentations or workshops with teachers/staff.

OUTLINE FOR TEACHER/STAFF CHECK-IN OR PRESENTATION

- Introduction.
- Explain your role.
- Inform the teacher/staff how long you will meet together (check-ins can occur within 10 to 15 minutes; presentations may last an hour or longer).
- Review the purpose of the meeting (see above).

1. Reactions

- Review common reactions of children and adults experiencing posttraumatic stress and grief.
- Review and provide educational information sheet. Information and handouts for teachers and staff about traumatic reactions to different types of trauma can be found at the National Child Traumatic Stress Network (see www.nctsnet.org), and for traumatic reactions that adults may have, see the National Center for PTSD (www.ptsd.va.gov). Highlight three common reactions, mentioning that if they have suffered from depression, anxiety, or substance abuse in the past they may be at a greater risk for worsening of symptoms or reoccurrence.
- Inform them about when to seek mental health intervention.

2. Responses

- Review some tips for coping.
- Encourage them to try at least two healthy coping strategies today and/or this week.
- Plan a specific day or time when they may implement these coping techniques.
- Inquire about the support they may need.
- Ask directly how the school or agency can provide support to them.
- Ask directly how the counselor or others can help.
- Record responses and plan follow-up check-in, if needed.

3. Relaxation

- Discuss the importance of taking the time to relax.

   a. Teach deep breathing exercises that they can use as well as ones that the children they work with can use.
   b. Discuss other positive relaxation strategies to help the body and mind calm down.

4. Resources

- Provide a list of community resources that includes information not only about city services, but also services such as mental health, substance abuse treatment, domestic violence, legal services, child care, etc.

TEACHER/STAFF SUPPORT: CHECK-IN PROTOCOL

Teacher/staff name: _____

Date and time of meeting: _____

Counselor: _____

Did you cover these topics? (check and note main topics/concerns)

❑ Introduction
❑ Common reactions

Notes:

_____

_____

❑ Coping tips

Notes:

_____

_____

❑ Support needed

Notes:

_____

_____

❑ Community resources

Follow-up:
Is a follow-up meeting needed? Yes or No
If yes, when is the best time to meet (list date, day, and time):

_____

Is follow-up action needed? Yes or No
If yes, what action needs to occur: _____

Notes:

_____

_____

REFERENCES

Mitchell, A. M., Wesner, S., Brownson, L., Dysart-Gale, D., Garand, L. & Havill, A. (2006). Effective communication with bereaved child survivors of suicide. *Journal of Child and Adolescent Psychiatric Nursing, 19*(3), 130–136. doi:10.1111/j.1744-6171.2006.00060.x

Chapter 6

GTI for Children Sessions

This chapter provides a protocol for when a child misses a session and a description of each session. The format is the same for each session: goals and tasks, tips, additional implementation notes, and a brief description of each session activity. In an effort to make this section user-friendly for the busy clinician, the session descriptions are succinct, yet provide enough information for the facilitator to understand how to implement the activity. Important reminders for ending GTI for Children are highlighted such as conducting the post-evaluations, providing progress information to parents/guardians and co-facilitators (as applicable), and making sure all final business has been addressed (e.g., ending with each child, reviewing the progress of each child, and determining whether any needed recommendations have been made).

PROCEDURES FOR MISSED SESSIONS

We want to try to minimize the number of times a child misses a session to ensure that the full grief and trauma intervention is provided to the child. Therefore, the procedures for missed sessions are as follows.

Specific Steps for Missed Sessions

1. If a child misses one of the first six scheduled group meetings (sessions 1–6), make up the missed session during the "pull-out" meeting by allowing additional time to cover the essential content that was missed.
2. If a child misses one of the last four scheduled group meetings (sessions 7–10), meet with the child individually to make up the essential content that was missed.

General Guidelines

1. As a general rule, when a child misses a session, meet with the child to find out why the session was missed (document the reason on the adherence checklist) and, if needed, problem-solve about ways to prevent this from happening in the future. For example, if the teacher did not allow the child to participate in the group meeting that day, talk with the teacher and explain the importance of attendance.

2. If a child does not attend a session, let the child know in the group meeting or individually that the child was missed and explain and/or have other group members explain to the child what they did during that session.

3. If a child misses *more than two group sessions*, consider calling the child's parent to see if the parent can encourage the child to attend, and talk with school personnel to ensure that the child attends the scheduled sessions.

4. Remember to give all parties involved a copy of the meeting times: this includes the parent, teacher or agency staff, secretary, principal, and the child.

NUMBER OF SESSIONS

If GTI for Children is being implemented in a group modality there is typically one parent meeting, one teacher/staff meeting (in a group or individually, if provided in a community-based setting), 10 group sessions, and one individual meeting with the child. Each group and individual session is typically one hour but, depending on the location, can range from 50 minutes to 1 hour and 15 minutes. If GTI for Children is provided individually or with a family, the number of sessions is the same, except one of the sessions could last a bit longer to address the information in the "pull-out" session, or this meeting can be held separately.

If a circumstance arises in which a child needs additional individual sessions or a family meeting (for example, if another death or traumatic event occurs), these should be provided as clinically indicated.

SESSION 1

Goals/tasks:

1. Establish purpose of intervention and if working in a group, have members introduce themselves.
2. Set rules. Explain confidentiality.
3. Increase comfort level and begin to build rapport and cohesion: ice breaker.
4. Acknowledge reason for participation in the intervention: have members *briefly* state why they are in the program (what happened, who died, losses, relationship to the deceased, and how they died).
5. Begin anger management/relaxation.
6. Identify at least one or two supportive adults.
7. Inquire about what the child enjoys doing.

> **TIP**
>
> Before coming to the meetings children may be participating in very different activities, such as math or physical exercise classes, or they may be coming straight from home. To help with the transition, it may be helpful to play relaxing music at the beginning until all the children are in the group. Calming music may help set the tone. It may help the children make the transition and help create emotional security within the group if you play the same music at the beginning of every session.

1. *Purpose and introduction:* When all the children have entered the group room, welcome them. Let them know that once they are all sitting down, the group will always start with a relaxation exercise and a light snack, and the facilitators will explain what they will be doing in the session for that day.

Facilitators should introduce themselves and ask the children to introduce themselves, stating their name and grade. Once the child has stated his or her name, he or she can write his/her name on a name tag and put it on.

Give the child(ren) a copy of the schedule of meetings. Let the children know that this is a special group that will only meet 10 times and that each child will meet one time individually with his or her counselor. Let them know that they will be doing different types of activities like drawing and playing with puppets, but that sometimes it might be hard for some of them to be in the group because of the purpose of the program. Explain that everyone in the group has had a hard time because of _____ (name the stressful events, for example, the disaster or the death of someone close), and the purpose of the group/intervention is to help them with their thoughts and feelings – in other words, to help them feel better inside.

If the group composition is heterogeneous in terms of the type of traumas experienced, facilitators may explain that "Everyone is in the group because they had something scary or sad happen" or "Everyone is in this group because they had something happen that is hard to talk about" or "Everyone is in this group because they have had something traumatic happen."

State that the purpose of the group is for everyone to share their thoughts and feelings about the scary or sad things that have happened so that they will feel better.

It is important to emphasize the purpose of the group in order to set the therapeutic tone of the group. Make sure the purpose is stated in the first three sessions.

2. *Rules:* It is important that this special group/intervention becomes a place where they feel safe to talk about their feelings and about what happened. Therefore, to be in the group/intervention, everyone has to agree to certain rules that will make the group or individual meeting time a special, safe place.

Facilitators ask each child what rule they would like to have in the group to make it a safe place to talk and share their feelings. Let every child state one rule. Impress upon them the importance of the rules. Then the facilitators add what they consider one of the most important rules: confidentiality. Explain the exceptions to confidentiality. Let them know that they can tell their parents what *they* said but not what other children said. The motto of the group is "what is said in group, stays in group" which means that children should not talk about what other children in the group said. When meeting with a child individually let him/her know that you will be sharing with his/her parent/caregiver about how the child is doing, and encourage him/her to talk with his/her parent/caregiver as well.

3. *Increase comfort level:* Have all of the children sit in a circle. Have each child develop a simple hand motion, body movement, or sound, for instance, clapping, snapping, stomping, or an easy dance-like movement with his or her hands or legs. Have children take turns saying their name and showing their "beat" (i.e., hand motion or sound). After each child does this, group members say, "okay _____ (name of child), we heard your beat," and all group members repeat it together. After every child has done this, have each child lead his/her beat and the group repeat it so that all that is heard is a continuous rhythm (beat). The group leader may want to use this exercise as a metaphor for a song by explaining that every beat and musician is important and unique when making a song and that sound is important and needs to be heard, just like all the members of this new group.

When meeting with a child individually, the clinician and the child both make up a two-step beat or body movement. Once these beats/moves have been shared, together they can be combined and repeated until a faster and then slower paced joint rhythm is established. The metaphor of working together and following each other's lead and pace can be discussed in terms of how the counseling will work.

Facilitators may use other ice breakers that help ease any anxiety, that are playful, and that help the children understand that the group members are to respect each other and offer support.

4. *Reason for participating:* Briefly remind all members again why they are in the group or meeting individually. Have each member briefly state why he or she is in the group or meeting individually. For example, "I am in the group, or I am here, because . . ." For some children it may be very difficult to even give a brief statement, for others it may be easier. Remind them

NOTE

Some children may be eager to talk about all of the gory, scary details. Other children may not be able to tolerate even mentioning what has happened to them. Since this is the first session, let children know that when they are feeling better they will have the opportunity to express themselves, but for now they will learn ways to feel calm and manage anger better. If a child begins to tell in detail about the scary trauma, gently stop him or her and let him or her know that you are really glad that he or she can talk about this. Let the entire group know that there will be a lot of time to talk about this later, but that first, everyone will need to learn ways to control their anger and to calm down.

that they will have more time to talk about this during another session, perhaps when they feel more comfortable.

5. *Anger management / relaxation*: This focuses on anger signs and relaxation. Explain that sometimes after something terrible happens, some children and adults may feel angry. Although this may be a normal response, it is important to express anger in a way that does not cause trouble to anyone. Give some suggestions as to why they may feel anger. For example, "some of you may feel angry because there have been too many changes since the disaster or because someone you love has died." Ask for other reasons why they may feel angry. Let them know that during this group or individually they will be working on ways to manage anger and that the first step is learning about anger signs that occur in our bodies. Identify the many ways that we can tell that children are angry by giving one or two suggestions (heart racing or clenched fist), and have each child identify his or her own anger sign and demonstrate it (act it out) to the group or to the clinician. You may ask the child(ren), "How can other people tell when you are mad?" Have children complete the "My Anger Signs" worksheet. Make this a fun activity by using drama to accentuate bodily reactions to anger. Ask them to try to notice when they feel this anger sign in their body.

TIP

Consider reading a short story about anger management during the first three sessions. There are many children's books on the market about anger that can be used. Two suggestions are: A. Moser (1994) *Don't rant and rave on Wednesdays!* and A. Moser (1988) *Don't pop your cork on Mondays!*

Teach deep breathing exercises (see "Two Step Relaxation" exercise instruction sheet). Ask them to do this before coming to the group each week. Explain that when they become upset this is one way to help the body calm down. Explain how important the deep breathing component of the exercise is and let them know that if they do not feel comfortable doing the entire exercise they should repeat the deep breathing (step 1) three times in a row. Teach them how to do this part by practicing it with them.

6. *Supportive adults:* Introduce book "My Story." Have children complete the title page and the first page about supportive adults. Discuss how important it is to have a caring adult who they feel comfortable talking with about their losses and feelings. Have each child think about who this might be for them and write down their name (see worksheet) and who they are in relation to the child. Encourage them to talk with this person about what they are doing in the group.

7. *Enjoyment / activities:* Through discussion, have the children identify things they enjoy doing for fun. Ask if they have been able to do this since the disaster, death, or traumatic event(s). If not, see if they can do it or, if that is not possible, discuss other things they can do that they enjoy. Let them know it is important to still take time and do things that are fun and that interest them because this can help them feel better. Encourage the children to become involved in extracurricular activities, especially sports. Inquire about children's involvement with physical activity as this is crucial for their mental health, health, and development. If clinicians can get children involved in other activities, this should be promoted.

Ending and announcements: Ask the group for ideas about a way to end the group. If they cannot agree on one idea, discuss this next time. Remind them about confidentiality.

Also, let the children know that meetings with parents will occur during which parents will learn about grief and trauma reactions too, be taught the deep breathing relaxation exercise, and get some general information about grief and trauma. Some children may become anxious about this meeting. Let them know that we find it helpful to meet with their parents so that they know everything that the child will be learning.

SESSION 2

Goals/tasks:

1. Review group goals.
2. Provide grief and trauma education.
3. Begin drawing and storytelling exercise. Give child option on topic: A Scary Thing Happened (trauma focused), I Really Miss (grief and loss focused), or When I Think About (name trauma or loss), I Think (grief focused).
4. Continue teaching anger management and relaxation.

Welcome everyone back and let them know how glad you are that they are in the group or back to meet individually. It is helpful to begin each group with everyone practicing deep breathing or another relaxation exercise. This can help calm everyone down before beginning and also reinforces the importance of relaxation. Also, if the group is being held in a school setting, it is helpful to play calming music as the children are entering the group setting so that they begin to calm down and also to help them make the transition from school to therapy.

1. *Purpose and goals:* Review the purpose of the group again. Review the goals with everyone and have them sign that they understand the goals (see "Goals" worksheet).

2. *Grief and trauma education:* Provide education about grief and trauma reactions. It is helpful to separate grief and traumatic responses into four different categories: (1) thoughts (grief: thoughts of missing the person; trauma: thoughts about how the person died); (2) feelings (grief: sad; trauma: intense anger); (3) body reactions (headaches, stomachaches, heart racing; feeling as if a traumatic moment is occurring again); (4) behaviors (grief: crying; trauma: angry outbursts resulting in temper tantrums or fighting). There is a grief and trauma wheel that is helpful to use as an illustration (see worksheet). It is important that the child understands how these reactions are all connected to how the child may be thinking, feeling (including body reactions), and acting.

Explain that all of these reactions are normal responses. Providing education about grief and trauma can be done using various approaches. For example, the facilitators may tell a story about a child (not in the group) who had someone close die and then review with the children, using the grief and trauma wheel, how this child may feel. It is recommended to use an example of another child and not use specific examples of each child's reactions until they learn more about grief and trauma and feel more comfortable in the group.

Another approach would be, while the children are eating the snacks, facilitators can write on a chalk board the four main categories of reactions and then ask children to offer suggestions of different types of reactions that may occur with each one. The facilitators can add to this list and provide explanations and examples of the reactions. Another approach to grief and trauma education utilizes puppets to express common grief and trauma reactions. Use of puppets to provide education is an engaging way for children to learn, especially for younger children. The facilitators act out with two puppets a child who is experiencing grief and traumatic reactions and an empathic adult who is listening, understanding, and acknowledging that these are normal responses. Cards with feeling expressions may also be used.

The children may also act out the reactions to situations of loss or upsetting situations provided by the clinician. In this exercise, the first child states a possible thought response, the next child acts out a feeling based on the thought, the next child demonstrates a bodily reaction, and the last child acts out the behavior. For example, the facilitator reads an example such as "Last night I heard that my grandparents would be moving to [name a place out of town that the children will recognize]." Have the first child state a thought in response to that statement, the next child act out the feeling, the next child act out the body reaction and the last child act out the behavior. Then ask the first child to change the thought and have the other children act out the corresponding feelings, body reactions and behaviors. Various teaching methods and resources that enhance learning (charts, drama, visual displays, and/or children's books on feelings) may be used.

3. *First storytelling exercise*: Explain that today and during the next seven sessions each child will have the opportunity to draw, tell a story about his or her drawing, and then write a story. All of the children's drawings and stories will be placed in their own special book entitled "My Story."

3a. *Introduce the "My Story" book.* Let the children know that they will be creating a special book and that at every session they will be working on a special worksheet that will become a part of their book. They can take home the book at the end. Allow the children time to color the title and add their names.

3b. To allow the child to have a sense of some control, the child can choose the topic. It is very important to allow the child to select the topic that he or she is most comfortable addressing and not to make the child tell his or her story. The child may also begin wherever he or she wishes in the chosen topic. Children still need to learn and practice relaxation techniques before going into any details of their traumatic loss. Therefore, it is important that children do not become overwhelmed or feel pressured during this activity. When discussing the drawing, only ask one or two questions. Do not probe or make the child tell the whole story. Praise them for what they shared and let them know that for some children it may be too soon to talk too much about what happened, but that later on, when they are ready and have learned more ways to calm down, they will have a chance to share more. We have found that by providing this early activity, which offers a snapshot about what happened, there is less avoidance when talking about the trauma later on, children understand the purpose of the treatment, and cohesion seems to build quicker.

The three worksheets the child can choose from are trauma, loss, and grief focused. If there is time remaining in another session, the child may complete the other two worksheets, if he or she wishes.

3c. Steps for narrative activities (draw, discuss, write, witness):

1. Child uses drawing to portray imagery of the identified topic.
2. Child and clinician discuss the drawing through a clinician-guided exploration of the child's thoughts, feelings, and perspective about the topic.
3. With the assistance of the clinician, the child writes the story about the topic.
4. A caring "outside witness" person and/or group of people listen to the child's story (Carr, 1998; White & Epston, 1990) while paying attention to and empathetically responding to the child's emotions.

NOTE

To help the children develop coherent narratives and to allow them to tell their story with rich descriptions and meaning, the activities are divided into four parts: drawing, in-depth discussion, a written narrative, and children should have an opportunity to share their thoughts and feelings with a caring person and/or group of people. After the children have finished the drawing, the clinician begins the conversation by stating, "So tell me/us about your drawing." The clinician follows by asking exploratory questions about thoughts and feelings. After the discussion, the clinician "plays secretary" and writes a story about the topic/drawing for the child on the "My Story" worksheet, unless the child wants to write it.

TIP

When children are writing, drawing, or creating something, let them know how much time will be allowed for the activity and then provide them with warnings about time ending. It is important that the child not experience frustration due to running out of time and not completing an activity. Therefore, if possible, allow as much time as the child needs. If this is not possible due to time constraints, provide the child with a lot of warnings and build in ways for him or her to complete the assignment. For example, "You have about ten more minutes to work on your story. You have five more minutes to work on your story. Okay, just about three more minutes. One more minute and we are going to have to end, but you can finish this later (next session or at home)." Some children may need constant reminders that their work is not part of school or an art class and that they do not need to worry about correct spelling or grammar or drawing the "perfect" picture. Remind them that what is important is that they are expressing their thoughts and feelings.

4. *Anger management/relaxation:* Focus here on anger signs but also on identifying anger triggers and learning ways to cool down. Cooling down from anger and learning to relax are to be discussed and practiced throughout the rest of the sessions (see worksheet).

Ask if the child noticed any of his/her anger signs this past week. Have the child briefly state (or if time allows, write down) the situation that precipitated the anger. "What anger sign did you notice? And what were you angry about?" Afterward explore options to help the child to calm down when he/she starts feeling the anger signs.

NOTE

To reinforce behavior of practicing anger management strategies, clinicians may give stickers or pencils to children who were able to recognize their anger signs. The following week if they practice one strategy to cool their anger, they will get another sticker or pencil. Have the children role-play using one of the strategies and ask them to try one of these strategies during the upcoming week when they notice their anger sign. Also, if deep breathing is not one of the chosen strategies, ask the children to keep practicing their deep breathing exercise. Ask if anyone did this last week. Ask them again to do it one time before the next session. Explain the importance of deep breathing.

Ending and announcements: End with the deep breathing exercise and a group ending ritual, if the group has developed one. Make sure the children know how many more times they will meet.

SESSION 3

Goal/tasks:

1. Continue with anger management.
2. Family support/changes.
3. Coping with anniversaries. This may be brought up again if a specific holiday occurs during group.
4. Spirituality/beliefs.

Welcome the children and explain the agenda for the day.

Offer a light snack.

Review the purpose of the group.

Explain what they will be doing in the group during this session.

Briefly review last session.

Ask if they can remember common grief and traumatic reactions and have the children review some of the reactions that were discussed last session.

Ask if the children can remember a time when they felt angry this past week. Did they notice their anger sign? Did they try one of the ways to calm or cool down?

NOTE

Clinicians may want to give stickers or pencils as a reward for practicing a cooling down strategy. As long as the child is working on utilizing these strategies, a reward may be given every session.

1. *Anger management*: Review that sessions 1 and 2 focused on identifying anger signs, identifying things that make you feel angry, and learning to calm down. Sometimes the situation that made the person feel angry can be handled in a positive manner (i.e., not by fighting, but by talking or removing oneself from the situation or ignoring the situation and calming down). Ask the child to give specific examples of a time in the past week or in the past month that he/she felt angry. Brainstorm with the child different ways the child could have reacted or behaved. Explore the consequences of each, and help the child decide which choices may have been acceptable approaches to addressing the situation. Caution: younger children may not be able to explore various approaches and to think through consequences. Also, sometimes the reason why children are angry, such as a loved one died or someone they loved was hurt, cannot be "fixed," but children can learn to recognize their anger, label exactly what makes them feel angry, and then find ways to feel better or ways to act that do not allow anger to get them into trouble. The time allowed for this topic depends on the amount of difficulty the child is having with managing his or her anger.

2. *Family support*: Have the child draw a picture of his or her family *and/or* about any changes since the traumatic event. Give children the choice of doing both drawings or only one. Once the drawing is complete, the clinician should say, "So tell me or the group about your drawing." The clinician follows by asking exploratory questions about the relationships of the child to different family members while probing to understand who provides emotional support to the child. Examples of questions are:

"So if you get really upset is there anyone that you would let know that you are upset?"
"Who makes you feel really safe (or comforted) to be around?"
"Of all of your family members, who knows when you are feeling sad?"
"Who do you get mad at the most, and why?"

After the discussion, the clinician "plays secretary" and writes a story about the drawing.

> **NOTE**
>
> It may be that a child has had a family member die and the child may need to draw or discuss more about the person who died, rather than other family members. If this is the case, the exploratory questions should focus on understanding the child's relationship with that person and about the deceased person's life. Children who have had a pet die may also need to talk about the loss of the pet.

3. *Anniversaries/holidays:* This topic may be brought up at another time during the 10 weeks to correspond with an anniversary that is approaching, or it may be addressed after the family support exercise. Discuss that anniversaries (date of death of the deceased) and holidays (Christmas, Kwanzaa, Easter, Thanksgiving, or other culturally specific days) may be a difficult time because of all of the changes since the loss. Ask if the child thinks this may be true for him or her, or if there is a certain holiday or anniversary that may be more difficult than others. Explore things that the child can do to help him or her cope with the anniversary/holiday. New or old rituals can be healing, and if the parent is available the clinician and child may want to talk about healing rituals that can occur. This also may be a good time to predict that during anniversaries or when a reminder occurs, old feelings and/or traumatic stress may be triggered and reoccur. The child should be reminded that if this happens, the child can practice coping strategies, like relaxation, learned during this intervention.

4. *Spirituality/beliefs:* The topic of spirituality may surface when talking about anniversaries, holidays, or ways of coping. If it does not, the clinician should bring it up. Spirituality can often be a source of strength for the child and family. However, this may not be true for everyone. Therefore, when talking about spirituality, it is important to respect different family beliefs and teachings. If the child has specific questions, such as "Why did God let this happen?" the clinician should praise the child for asking the question and have the child identify someone in his or her family who he or she feels comfortable discussing this with. The child can write his or

her question down and take it to that person. If time permits, the child is encouraged to draw or write a prayer, poem, or song (see worksheets) and share it with the group and/or clinician.

Ending and announcements: End with the deep breathing exercise and a group ending ritual if the group has developed one. Make sure the children know how many more times they will meet.

SESSION 4

Goals/tasks:

1. Feelings. Use puppets to role-play feelings. Show how to express or handle feelings, especially feelings of avoidance, re-experiencing, and being scared. Teach strategies for coping with re-experiencing the traumatic event. Continue education on grief and traumatic feeling reactions.
2. Explore questions.

Welcome the children and explain the agenda for the day.
Offer a light snack.
Explain what they will be doing in the group during this session.
Briefly review last session.
Ask if the children practiced relaxation exercises or were able to recognize anger signs or use cool down strategies. Give sticker or pencil as a reward, and encourage them to continue to use these techniques.

1. *Feelings:* Review the list of feelings that were discussed in session 2 by having the child or children think about and list different feelings when a child has been through something traumatic and/or is grieving. Using drama, have the child act out or demonstrate how his or her face may look if he or she is feeling scared, angry, sad, worried, guilty, brave, confused, or happy. In a group setting, the child can act out one of the feelings and then have the other children guess the feeling. In an individual meeting, the child and clinician can take turns using facial expression to act out the feeling. Afterward, explain how common these feelings are after something terrible has happened. If the child is not comfortable "acting," it may be helpful to use creative materials (feeling faces cards or posters, or books about feelings) to illustrate different feelings. Clinicians should take extra time to explore feelings of *worry* and *guilt* as these two emotions may be the result of misinformation and distortion.

    The clinician should also talk about common traumatic responses such as avoidance (not wanting to be reminded) and re-experiencing (intrusive thoughts and images, etc.). Have each child indicate which feeling or feelings he/she has been experiencing the most lately. Have the child draw him or herself feeling the identified way. Discuss with the child the drawing while asking probing questions (e.g., "How long have you been feeling this way? Who knows that you have been feeling this way? What would we need to do so that you didn't worry about that? Is there someone in your family that you could show this picture to and talk about how you have been feeling?"). Write the child's story about the drawing.

2. *Questions:* Sometimes discussion of feelings is accompanied by the feeling of confusion. Feeling confused may be the result of misinformation or of simply trying to understand the magnitude of what has happened. Children need to be allowed to ask questions and to be given honest information in an age-appropriate manner. Let the children know that if they have any questions, they may ask them. Encourage children with questions to write them down. Sometimes children's questions do not have easy answers. It is okay to let the child know that

you are not sure of the answer, and it may be that the caregiver needs to become involved in helping to answer the child's question, especially if the question challenges one of the family's beliefs. At the end of this activity children may want to express what they wish would have happened (past) and/or what they wish will happen (present and future). If time allows, have the child complete the "I Wish" worksheet and follow the protocol of drawing, discussing, writing, and witnessing.

NOTE

Clinicians may use this time to explain and discuss with children specific topics related to the traumatic event. For example, if the traumatic event was a hurricane, children may benefit from information about hurricane warnings and evacuations, or if a violent death occurred, information about suicide or court proceedings for a murder trial may need to be discussed. Allow the child(ren) to guide the discussion, and remember to give information in a developmentally appropriate manner.

Ending and announcements: End with the deep breathing exercise and a group ending ritual if the group has developed one. Remind child(ren) to identify anger signs and practice cool down strategies including relaxation. Make sure the children know how many more times they will meet.

TIP

Hopefully by this time the child's anxiety about participating has decreased. However, some children may still be unsure if they want to continue and may feel scared about knowing that eventually they will be telling more of their story about what happened. Therefore, clinicians need to constantly work on helping to make the child feel comfortable, and one of the best ways to do this is through play. Use of play is also a good coping technique for children. If time permits, add fun by ending the session with a simple, non-stressful game, for instance, the game UNO. Avoid playing complex games that create frustration and that set up competition within the group because generally there will not be sufficient time to solve the social conflicts that result.

SESSION 5

Goals/tasks:

1. Explore dreams: comforting dreams and nightmares.
2. Discuss issues of safety: define what it means to feel safe, draw safe place or person, relaxation exercise, guided imagery to a safe place.

Welcome the children and explain the agenda for the day.
Offer a light snack.
Explain what they will be doing in the group during this session.
Ask if the children practiced relaxation exercises or were able to recognize anger signs or use
    cool down strategies. Give sticker or pencil as a reward, and encourage them to continue
    to use these techniques.

1. *Dreams*: Explain that there are many different types of dreams and after something really terrible happens, our dreams may change. Some dreams can make us feel good or comforted and other dreams can be really scary, like nightmares. Ask if the child has noticed having any different type of dream since the trauma/loss. Ask if the dream made him/her feel good or scared him/her. Explore if there are signs of *hope or bravery* in the child's dream.

> **NOTE**
>
> Some children may not have night-time dreams, but have had or are having daydreams that are scary or that involve fantasies about what they wish would have happened. If a child says he or she does not have dreams, ask about daydreams. However, use caution when children start telling daydreams that are actually fantasies, especially when the fantasy seems to be a mixture of different traumatic aspects. It may be that the child is experiencing great confusion about what actually happened and perhaps clarification and/or communication with a caring adult family member to help the child clarify misinformation is needed. If the child does not seem to have active dreams, continue with the next activity.

If the dream made them feel good, have the child draw about the dream, discuss the drawing, and have the child write a story about it.

If the dream was scary for him/her, have the child draw about it, discuss the drawing, and then before writing a story about it, allow the child to try to add to the dream to make it not so scary. For example, have the child draw his or her scary picture. Say, "So tell me about your drawing." If a child had a scary dream, ask, "What would make it not so scary?" or "How could it end where you would feel good?" and/or have the child draw something in the original picture that changes it so that it is not scary. Next, have the child write about the drawing. The story should include both the scary dream and the changed story that made him or her feel better or not too scared.

Since many school-age children dream about monsters, finish this exercise by reading the book, *Go Away Big Green Monster* (Emberly, 1993).

TIP

If the child reports that he or she is having a lot of nightmares and/or not sleeping well, a parent meeting may be indicated. Disruption of sleep can lead to significant problems in several areas of a child's life. Hopefully, with the assistance of the intervention, which allows the child the opportunity to express him or herself, sleeping will improve. If the child reports that she or he is still having severe disruptions in sleep that have not improved since the intervention began, consider another parent meeting to discuss tips for improved sleeping. Some sleeping tips include limiting caffeine, establishing calming and nurturing bedtime routines (such as parent cuddling with his or her child and reading a favorite (not scary) bedtime story), eating healthy meals and snacks, and getting exercise. Ask the parent to monitor the child's sleep and to report back on progress and/or concerns.

2. *Safety:* Safety is addressed in a three-part exercise: (1) defining safety, (2) drawing a safe place or person, and (3) sensing feeling safe through a guided meditation.

Ask the children if they know what feeling safe means. Help them to define feeling safe. Write down the definitions. Ask about safety in different contexts. For example, where do they feel safe – at home, at school, in their community?

Have the child draw about feeling safe. Let the child choose from the three worksheets: "My Safe Place," "My Safe Person," or "My Protective Shield." Note, in the case of a disaster, some children may have lost the place that feels safe to them and may not have reestablished a new place. If this is the case, they can either make up a safe place or perhaps complete the safety protection shield worksheet. Also, after children identify one safe place or safe person, have them think about their ecological context and list safe places or people in each area such as at home, at school, or in the neighborhood.

Guided imagery: begin with a deep breathing exercise and facilitate guided imagery about feeling safe. See the example of a guided imagery exercise located in the Appendix.

Ending and announcements: Inform the children in the group that after the next session, the clinician will meet individually with them. If there are two clinicians and only one will be meeting with the child, let them know that only one clinician will be meeting with the child so that he or she is not disappointed when both are not present.

End with the deep breathing exercise and a group ending ritual if the group has developed one. Remind child(ren) to identify anger signs and practice cool down strategies including relaxation. Make sure the children know how many more times the group will meet.

TIP

Clinicians should review each child's Clinical Chart before session 6 to make sure that the clinician is reminded of the child's most salient events and so that the clinician can guide the child to address these events in the upcoming sessions.

SESSION 6

Goals/tasks:

1. To create a coherent narrative: about before, during, and after what happened.
2. End with relaxation.

> **TIP**
>
> Before conducting this session, read the agenda for session 6, the "pull-out" session, and session 7 because they all focus on the same topic.

Welcome the children and explain the agenda for the day.
Offer a light snack.
Explain what they will be doing in the group during this session.
Ask if the children practiced relaxation exercises or were able to recognize anger signs or use cool down strategies. Give sticker or pencil as a reward, and encourage them to continue to use these techniques.

> **TIP**
>
> Before conducting this activity with the child, review the Clinical Chart form and initial meeting form as a reminder of the child's trauma and losses. Children may try to avoid these identified events and tell a less frightening story. Knowing that he or she has strengths and has developed new coping strategies from participating in the previous sessions encourages the child to tell his or her story about the traumatic event. What the child shares and where the child starts and stops is up to the child, but with caring guidance, the clinician will help the child tell his or her story with a full description and lessened feelings of fear.

Coherent narrative: Session 6, the "pull-out" session (March et al., 1998), and session 7 focus on helping the child to create a coherent narrative about what happened. To assist the child to create a fuller story, three worksheets are used which guide the child through drawing/discussing what occurred before, during, and after the traumatic event.

This narrative account with three parts allows the child to begin where he or she is able to start. For example, it may be that a child who has had someone close die may want to spend more time on the "Before It Happened" worksheet where memories of fun times and the closeness of the relationship can be recalled and shared with the clinician and other group participants before the story of how the person died is told. However, another child may start with the beginning of the dying story, starting the account right before the person died. Give the child the freedom to choose where to begin and end, but it is imperative that before this activity takes place the child has ample coping strategies so that he or she can tell his or her story.

Time should be taken with the narrative component, which is why three sessions are devoted to completing the worksheets "Before," "During," "Worst Moment," and "After." It is recommended that the before and during stories be completed in session 6, the worst moment in the "pull-out" session, and the after it happened in session 7. For each part the draw, discuss, write, and witness process is used. However, it is recommended that the worst moment only be shared in the individual session so that other children are not hearing and seeing the often gruesome traumatic content.

After the child draws imagery, the facilitator is to listen to the child describe his or her story. The facilitator says, "So tell me about your drawing." While listening to the child, the facilitator will follow up with important clinical questions that will help the child to understand themselves better in the context of the story and to begin to put together a coherent narrative. This type of exploration is based on the restorative retelling techniques developed by E. K. Rynearson (see Rynearson, 2001).

There are four main types of questions:

1. Relationship questions such as why was this person special to you, what would they say to you now, what would you like to say to them now, or who do you have now in your life that provides support to you?
2. Context questions such as where were you when this occurred, what do you remember hearing, seeing, smelling, or when did this happen?
3. Individual-focused questions such as how were you feeling, what were you thinking, what was occurring within your body, or what are you thinking and feeling now, and do you have any body reactions that you are experiencing right now?
4. Furthering questions such as what happened next, what else did you see, what else were you thinking or feeling, and will you please tell me more about that?

Other questions may include:

Before it happened:
How is this person special to you?
What's happening?
How did you feel when you were with this person?
What did you like to do with her or him? Where did you like to go together?
What did you learn from this person?
What do you want us to remember about your loved one?
Tell me more about what this time was like for you.
Did you see yourself differently then? If so, how?
What do you think was occurring then?

When it happened:
Where did this happen? Describe the scene.
Were you there when it happened? If not, when did you find out that it happened?

What do you wish you could've done?

What do you wish you could've said?

What was it like for you to do this drawing?

Worst moment:

Where did this happen? Describe the scene.

Of this scene, what bothers you the most, what is the hardest to talk about?

What would you have liked to be able to tell others about this worst moment?

What would (name the deceased person) tell you about this moment and what would you like to say to him or her?

How was it for you to talk about it?

After it happened:

What would (insert the deceased person's name) want for you now?

If your loved one were here with you right now, imagine what he/she would do to help you or what he/she would say to you.

How do you see yourself after this happened?

Afterward, the child is to write a story ("My Story") about the drawings. Usually only one story is written about what happened, which will include what was drawn and discussed in the three worksheets.

TIP

Some children may not like to draw; for some children having to complete three worksheets is too much. Therefore, as an alternative, clinicians may want to use only the one worksheet entitled "What Happened" and focus less on drawing and more on discussion. This decision should be tailored to the child's needs.

Clinicians should listen for signs of *bravery and hope* and highlight these instances. It may be that this alternative story of bravery and hope needs to be given more attention. Allow the child the time to tell this story and draw about it if he/she wishes. (The worksheet "Another Important Story" may be used during this time, or any time during the counseling.)

NOTE

Considerable time should be spent on this exercise. Therefore, if needed, the "Afterward," or "After the Disaster" drawing/discussion/writing may be completed in the seventh session. Usually the sharing within the group will take place in session 7 once children have had a chance to work on the completion of this activity.

TIP
—

If scheduling conflicts do not allow for a "pull-out" session, clinicians may lengthen session 6 to include the activities in the "pull-out" session. However, when this intervention is being used in a group modality, one individual session (i.e., "pull-out" session) is recommended so that the unique needs of the child can be addressed. Also some children may finish this exercise quicker than others; therefore, when a child finishes and is waiting on the others, have him or her spend some time decorating his or her book by coloring in all of the titles; ask the child to draw another story (an alternative story) about what happened; or have him or her complete one of the worksheets that he or she did not choose to do in an earlier session. Free play time is not recommended for the children who finish earlier than the others because the other children may rush through the exercise so that they can play instead.

Ending and announcements: To help moderate any distress, this session should end with the relaxation exercise and the child should be encouraged to practice it every day during the week. A reward of stickers or pencils may be offered next session for practicing. Inform the children in the group that the clinician(s) will meet individually with them.

ADDITIONAL INDIVIDUAL "PULL-OUT" (AFTER SESSION 6)

Research from prior GTI for Children groups revealed that child participants missed 12 percent of the scheduled sessions (mean number of missed sessions 1.28). Therefore, to provide additional therapeutic intervention and to address the unique needs of group members, a "pull-out" session, similar to the approach developed by March and associates (1998), is provided to each group member. The "pull-out" session can also be used as a "make-up" session to ensure that the child addresses all of the topics.

> **NOTE**
>
> For children receiving GTI for Children individually, these topics may be addressed in session 6. However, if the child has a difficult time remaining focused, conduct this meeting as an additional session.

This session is to be tailored to the needs of the child. However, below are some suggested topics to address during this time.

1. If the child was absent during any of the first six sessions, address the essential topic(s) that were not covered.
2. Review story of what happened (of what was completed in session 6).
3. *Worst moment or part:* Children are encouraged to confront their worst moment of the experience rather than avoid talking about it. Clinicians need to provide extra support during this exercise. Creating the narrative by having the child explore the beginning, middle, and end may take most of the group session. Therefore, the worst moment exercise can be completed in the individual "pull-out" session. Exploring this individually rather than within the group may also prevent re-traumatizing other children by sharing these stories. When seeing children individually, clinicians should continue with this session and explore the worst moment of the child's experience.

   This exercise follows the draw, discuss, and write format, except after each step clinicians need to check-in with the child to see how distressed they are feeling. For example, after they finish the drawing, ask "How upset are you feeling right now after drawing your worst moment? None, a little, some, or a whole lot?" Continue with having the child discuss the drawing ("So tell me") and then afterward ask "How upset are you feeling right now after talking about your worst moment?" After the child or the clinician/secretary writes about the worst moment, have the child rate how upset he/she feels. Hopefully, by the third time reviewing the worst moment the child will not feel as distressed.
4. Address the child's feelings of guilt. Ask direct probing questions such as "Do you think you did something to cause this terrible thing to happen? Do you think anyone is mad at you because of what happened? Are you mad at anyone because of what happened?" This direct exploration about guilt is from the Preschool PTSD Treatment manual (Scheeringa, Amaya-Jackson & Cohen, 2002).

5. Explore if the child is exposed to trauma reminders. If so, discuss coping strategies, especially ways the child can cope when he/she is confronted with trauma reminders in his or her everyday routine.
6. Reinforce use of relaxation. Practice individually with the child.
7. Address any unique needs of the child.

NOTE

Having one individual session while using the group modality may interfere with group processes. For instance, children may wait to share intense emotions individually rather than in a group, or children may rely only on the clinician for support and not the other children. Therefore, it is important to challenge children (when appropriate) to share with the group what they discussed individually with the facilitators in the "pull-out" meeting. However, some issues may be addressed individually, such as if a child discloses that he or she was abused.

SESSION 7

Goals/tasks:

1. Complete coherent narrative.
2. Promote coping and seeking support.

Welcome the children and explain the agenda for the day.
Offer a light snack.
Explain what they will be doing in the group during this session.
Ask if the children practiced relaxation exercises or were able to recognize anger signs or use
    cool down strategies. Give sticker or pencil as a reward, and encourage them to continue
    to use these techniques.

1. *Complete what happened narrative*: Spend time on completing the activities from session 6 so that a complete narrative has been reviewed. Clinicians may want to have children share (when appropriate) what they discussed in the individual sessions. This works best if there was a common theme that was brought up by the children in the individual sessions. For example, if some of the children reported that they felt guilty, clinicians may want to bring this topic up for further group discussion to help normalize the feeling, provide more education about grief and trauma, and to allow further time to process the theme. Allow some time for sharing and discussion.

2. *Coping and supports:* Discuss the need for children to have many ways that they cope (or deal) with what has happened. Having only one main coping mechanism is not sufficient and it may lead to a decrease in functioning. Therefore, each child is encouraged to have at least five main ways of helping him or herself feel better.

Have the child or the group members list positive things they can do to feel better, and write them down. From this list, have the child identify at least five things he/she can do. *During this activity, predict re-occurrences of distress and encourage use of new skills and coping.* Let them know that while they may be feeling better now, old feelings about what happened may come back, especially during holidays or anniversary times. For example, next year during hurricane season children may need to be educated about the timing of hurricane season and how usually the National Hurricane Center is able to warn people days in advance. When these old feelings return they can use their coping list.

It is important that at least one of the things they list includes talking with a supportive person. Encourage the child to identify the person (this was also done in session 2) and include this coping strategy on his or her list. Ask him or her to do at least one of these things this week to feel better.

NOTE

To encourage the child to keep the coping list, it is recommended that the clinician make the list special by taking a copy of the list and re-typing and personalizing it with the child's name typed and clip art added, or putting the list in a clear frame and allowing the child to paint a border on the frame, or by having special paper for the child to write their list or make a fun colorful collage with all the ways of coping. *Clinicians are encouraged to make this activity special and creative so that the children can feel proud of their work and to encourage children to keep the list.*

Ending and announcements: End with the deep breathing exercise and remind them to practice cooling down when they feel anger signs. If a closing ritual was developed, end with the ritual. Remind group members about confidentiality. Let them know how many meetings are remaining.

SESSION 8

Goals/tasks:

1. Memories of loss(es)/deceased.
2. Meaning of loss(es)/relationship to deceased.

Welcome the children and explain the agenda for the day.
Offer a light snack.
Explain what they will be doing in the group during this session.
Ask if the children practiced relaxation exercises or if they tried anything from their coping list that they developed in session 7. Ask for specific examples. Give sticker or pencil as a reward, and encourage them to continue to use these coping methods.
Return the "cool" typed or perhaps framed copy of the child's coping list that was developed in session 7.

1. *Memories:* Have the child choose one of the four worksheets (entitled "The Thing I Miss the Most," "My Favorite Memory," "A Happy Time Together," or "My Story About _____") and draw a picture. (Note: if the child has already completed the "I Really Miss" worksheet from session 2, have them complete one of the other worksheets.)

2. *Meaning:* To explore the meaning of the child's loss(es) (and/or if someone close has died, the relationship between the child and the deceased), spend time allowing the child to share with the other group members and clinician about his/her loss(es). For children who have ambivalent feelings or negative feelings toward the person who died, the worksheet "My Story About _____" may be used. Also, in situations where the loss is not due to a death but due to other losses such as moving to a new neighborhood or school, or a change in living arrangements, other types of losses can be discussed.

The clinician or group members may ask questions to help them understand the meaning of the loss(es). For example:

"Tell us more about things you used to do with (the deceased)?"
"What will you miss the most about (your house, your pet, etc.)?"
"What was so special to you about (name the loss)?"
"What one thing would you want other people to know about (name the loss)?"
"How do you think your loss has affected you?"

Afterward, help the child write a story ("play secretary") about the drawing.

Planning the celebration, ending, and announcements: Before ending, take extra time to praise the child for talking about what happened and expressing his or her thoughts and feelings. Let him/her know that a celebration will be held at the last session and ask what type of special food the child would like. However, it is best to give the child a choice of what type of food the clinician is willing to bring to the last session (often this depends on the clinician's budget and time available to get the food). Allow time for children to express their thoughts about ending.

End with the deep breathing exercise and remind them to practice cooling down when they feel anger signs. If a closing ritual was developed, end with the ritual. Remind the group members about confidentiality. Let them know how many meetings are remaining.

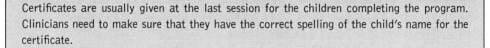

TIP

Certificates are usually given at the last session for the children completing the program. Clinicians need to make sure that they have the correct spelling of the child's name for the certificate.

SESSION 9

Goals/tasks:

1. Positive comforting memories.
2. Focus on the positive (clinical decision as to completing during this session or session 10).
3. Discuss ending.
4. Review goals now or during the post-evaluation period.

Welcome the children and explain the agenda for the day.
Offer a light snack.
Explain what they will be doing in the group during this session.
Ask if the children used any of the things on their list of things they can do to feel better. Give
   sticker or pencil as a reward, and encourage them to continue to use these techniques.

1. *Positive comforting memories:* This session allows additional time for children to talk about their loss(es) and share their experiences. Children may want to complete the other worksheets from session 8. If the child shared more ambivalence about the loss or negative feelings, spend this time helping the child to process his or her thoughts and feelings about the loss.

2. *Focus on the positive:* The future activity is to help the child see hope in the future, and to become aware of any positive aspects of their situation. All children should be praised for their bravery for completing all of the past activities and talking about their thoughts and feelings. Have children complete one of the worksheets entitled "My Hope for the Future" or "Things About My Life That I Like" by drawing their response, discussing it, and then writing a story about it. When the child is discussing his or her drawing, the clinician should ask exploratory questions to elicit positive visions of the future or positive aspects of the child's current situation. One of the goals is to have the child express some optimism about his or her current situation.

NOTE

If time allows, have the child complete both of these worksheets. If the child(ren) need more time with the memories worksheets, they may be completed in session 10, but it is better to save session 10 for celebration and not working on worksheets if possible.

---

3. *Ending:* Discuss that there will be one more meeting of the group after this session, or that children being seen individually will only meet one more time. Let them know that they will have a celebration and receive a certificate for completing the 10 sessions. Also, plan the special type of snacks that the children want to have for the celebration. Clinicians should lead a discussion about how hard it may be for some to end and about the feelings of sadness or anger that may surface, but should also discuss the positive benefits of attending the sessions and the children's new skills of coping with sadness and anger.

4. *Goal review:* It is best to meet with each child individually after session 10 for an evaluation session. If time permits, conduct the goal review in the individual meeting. However, if not, it is better to complete this during session 9 rather than waiting until session 10 when the child may not feel like taking the time in the last session to review the goals.

NOTE

If there is time remaining in this session, allow children to review prior completed work and finish any uncompleted worksheets that they began in another session. Making sure that all of the worksheets that the child works on are completed will help the child feel a sense of accomplishment and it may make it easier for the child to end.

After session 9 organize the child's book so that it is ready for the child to take home after session 10. Clinicians may want to type the child's narrative that was written for each worksheet so that the typed story accompanies each drawing. Go ahead and insert the last worksheet (see session 10 worksheets) and have the book bound. Use either a three-hole folder, or if funds permit, have the book spiral bound.

Ending and announcements: End with the deep breathing exercise and remind them to practice cooling down when they feel anger signs. If a closing ritual was developed, end with the ritual. Remind group members about confidentiality. Remind the children again that there is one more meeting.

SESSION 10

Goals/tasks:

1. Focus on the positive (if not completed in session 10).
2. Reconnecting.
3. Review and celebrate progress.
4. Say goodbye.

Welcome the children and explain the agenda for the day.
Explain what they will be doing in the group during this session.
Enjoy special food (and music if the children want).

1. *Focus on the positive:* If this activity was not completed in session 9, please have the children complete one of the two worksheets entitled "My Hope for the Future" or "Things About My Life That I Like" or both if time allows. The goal is to have the child express some optimism about his or her future or current situation.

2. *Reconnecting:* Throughout this intervention one focus has been on having the child identify supportive people. It is important that the children share what they have been doing in this program with the supportive adult(s). Read aloud the last worksheet, and explain that their book, "My Story," is not completed until it has been shared with and signed by their caring safe person.

   Also, in session 1 and during the assessment each child identified things that they enjoyed doing. If the child is not engaged in recreational activities and/or does not have things that he or she enjoys doing, make every effort to spend time with the child helping him/her along with his/her caregiver(s) to get connected with people and activities that can bring periods of relief and, hopefully, fun and enjoyable times.

3 and 4. *Review, celebrate, and say goodbye:* Conduct a formal ceremony with the clinician presenting a certificate to the children and praising them for their accomplishments during the 10 sessions. Give children the opportunity to say something about what they learned from the group or how they benefited, or anything else they want to share with the other group members. Present to each child a participation certificate and his or her personal copy of the "My Story" book. It is important to encourage children to share their books with caring adults, especially their primary caregivers.

ENDING GTI FOR CHILDREN

Group Facilitators Meeting

Clinicians who are conducting community-based groups should have one final meeting scheduled one week later, at the same time and in the same location as the group meeting. This scheduled meeting can be used to meet with any child who may have missed the last group, to review each group member's progress and future needs, and/or to follow up with any community members who may have helped to organize the group.

Post-Evaluation

The assessment measures that were administered before GTI for Children was provided should be administered after the intervention. The same procedures that were followed during the pre-assessment should be followed. For instance, the same evaluator should administer the surveys, the evaluation should occur in the same location if possible, and the instruments should be administered in the same order and in the same way. In addition, the Grief and Trauma Intervention for Children Review of Goals survey provided in the Appendix should be included in the post-evaluation.

Once the post-evaluation is completed, the group facilitator or clinician who provided GTI for Children should be provided with the evaluation so that each child's progress is reviewed and parents are informed about the results. If possible, it is helpful to conduct a follow-up assessment 3 to 6 months after participation in GTI for Children, to see if treatment gains have been maintained.

Post-Intervention Contact with Parent

At the end of the intervention, the clinician should contact the parent(s) to inform him/her that the intervention has been completed and to review the progress of his/her child as well as provide any needed recommendations and/or referrals. Talk with the parent(s) about helping the child with any upcoming anniversaries or holidays such as hurricane season or the deceased's birthday. Encourage the parent(s) to praise his or her child for completing GTI for Children. Also, provide the parent(s) with a summary of the evaluation results. If the child remains in the clinically symptomatic range on any of the measures, suggest to the parent(s) that additional therapy be sought for the child and provide a list of resources for counseling. Provide any other recommendations that may be warranted.

REFERENCES

Carr, A. (1998). Michael White's narrative therapy. *Contemporary Family Therapy, 20*, 485–503.

Emberly, E. (1993). *Go away big green monster*. New York: Little, Brown Books for Young Readers.

March, S. M., Amaya-Jackson, L., Murray, M. C. & Schulte, A. (1998). Cognitive-behavioral psychotherapy for children and adolescents with posttraumatic stress disorder after single-incident stressor. *Journal of the American Academy of Child and Adolescent Psychiatry, 37*(6), 585–593. doi:10.1097/00004583-199806000-00008

Moser, A. (1988). *Don't pop your cork on Mondays!* Kansas City, MO: Landmark Editions, Inc.

Moser, A. (1994). *Don't rant and rave on Wednesdays*! Kansas City, MO: Landmark Editions, Inc.

Rynearson, R. (2001). *Retelling violent death*. Philadelphia: Brunner-Routledge.

Scheeringa, M. S., Amaya-Jackson, L. & Cohen, J. (2002). *Preschool PTSD treatment*. New Orleans, LA.

White, M. & Epston, D. (1990). *Narrative means to therapeutic ends*. New York: W. W. Norton & Company.

Chapter 7

GTI for Children in Action

This chapter presents common questions or experiences that clinicians have when implementing GTI for Children. This chapter provides a discussion of and possible solutions to common clinical implementation issues. Case vignettes from clinicians who have implemented GTI for Children are used to provide the reader with more insight into how these issues may be addressed and to give the reader an understanding of what may occur when implementing GTI for Children.

COMMON QUESTIONS, RESPONSES, AND VIGNETTES

1. What do I do if I am not able to cover all of the topics for the assigned session?

Sometimes you may not be able to cover all of the topics in the assigned session. If this occurs, it is helpful to review why this occurred so that you can see if this was just a one-time occurrence or if it will most likely continue to occur. For example, were the topics not covered because the group or individual session started late due to unforeseen circumstances that are not likely to happen again, or were they not covered because the facilitator is having a difficult time helping the children transition from one topic to the next and is not managing the time? The first step is to explore the reasons why this occurred and then problem-solve. The second step would be to think about how the missed information could be addressed in the next session. If possible, maybe 15 minutes could be added to the next session to allow more time to complete the missed topic and the current session topics, or maybe one topic in the next session gets started and then children can work at their own pace to complete it. On occasion, it is possible to send the worksheets home with the children, but this is not generally recommended. If group members are asked to complete the worksheet at home, it is highly likely that one or some of the children may not complete it and then the clinician is still faced with how this material will be addressed for the one child. Also, the children who did not complete the worksheet often feel left out of the discussion when the topic is addressed in the session. When seeing a child individually, this may be a good option to have the child complete the worksheet for homework, but in a group setting the children who did not complete the worksheet are often then left out of the discussion and sharing on the topic.

2. What happens when the child expresses guilt about what happened in the first two sessions?

Guilt and blame are directly discussed in session 4 and in the individual "pull-out" session with the child. However, these themes may arise early, especially if the child feels that what happened was his/her fault or if he/she blames others for what happened. Guilt and blame are often intense feelings and usually take some time for the child to process and change his/her thoughts and feelings. These two feelings may be shared early in the intervention, such as when spirituality and beliefs are being discussed in session 3 or when anger management is discussed in session 1 when the child writes about why he/she feels angry. Since the child has not learned all of the coping skills or had a chance to share his/her trauma narrative, it is best to empathetically listen and then, at a later time, such as in the individual "pull-out" session, explore further these thoughts and how the child may understand his/her role and that of others differently. When GTI for Children is provided in a group setting it is common for the other children to provide some reflective comments about their feelings back to the child.

Vignette: Session 3: topic not covered and guilt expressed

During session 3, the facilitator spent a lot of time addressing anger management strategies since several of the group members had been suspended for fighting in school. As a result, the facilitator was not able to address the topic of spirituality. Usually, facilitators cover unaddressed topics in the next session. However, since the group members had been very engaged in and liked the drawing activities, the facilitators decided to let the children take home the three spirituality worksheets ("My Prayer," "My Song," and "My Poem"). The facilitators told the children to try to complete one of the worksheets before the next session. The facilitators gave the group members special colored folders to put the worksheets in, so that they did not lose the worksheets, and to keep these papers separate from their school work. The following week, five of the children brought back a completed worksheet and one child did not. The facilitators assured the one child that there would be time later to complete the worksheet or he could take the worksheet home again. The child took the worksheet home again but did not bring it back. The facilitator addressed the topic of spirituality and beliefs during the individual "pull-out" session with the child.

One of the children, Tyrone (age 7), brought in a poem that he had written and he read it aloud to everyone in the group. After he shared his poem, the facilitators explored its meaning with him. Tyrone reported that he believed his thoughts had caused Hurricane Katrina. He couldn't explain exactly why he thought this, but he clearly believed it and exhibited fear that he had caused such destruction. The facilitators asked the other group members what they thought. Did they think Tyrone had caused the hurricane because of his thoughts? They all responded "no way," "you couldn't cause that," "it was nature," "there's no way your thoughts could have caused all that destruction." Tyrone listened but was still unsure. In the individual "pull-out" session the facilitator asked Tyrone again if he thought he had caused the hurricane to happen. He shared that since he talked about his thoughts that he caused the hurricane to happen, he had heard his family and others in the neighborhood discuss several reasons why it occurred, such as God is punishing people for being bad, it was just "mother nature," and these types of bad storms happen and have happened over the history of time. He even heard a discussion about how the destruction occurred due to the levees breaking. Tyrone learned more about hurricanes and was able to acknowledge that the hurricane was not his fault.

Vignette: Sessions 1, 4, and 6: thoughts and feelings of guilt are explored

During session 1, when group members were asked to briefly state why they were in the group, Brian, a 7-year-old boy, alluded to his father blaming him for the death of his 1-year-old sister who choked to death after swallowing a screw she had picked up from the ground. Brian stated, "I did not pick up the screws that were on the ground and my sister died. My dad told me I should have picked up the screws." During session 4 when discussing feelings, Brian directly expressed his guilt for not having picked up the screws. Brian, who appeared very sad, whispered quietly but loud enough so that all group members could hear him, "It's my fault. I should have picked up the screws." Sadie listened carefully to Brian and could tell how bad he felt. Sadie told him, "Brian, it was an accident. It is not your fault." Juan, an 8-year-old boy, quickly added, "You are just a kid. I don't always pick up my toys when I am supposed to. The adults in the home should have picked up the screws." All of the other group members agreed that Brian's sister's death was not Brian's fault, and the group facilitators told him this as well.

Brian seemed to feel much better letting everyone know how he had been thinking and feeling, and the group members helped him to start thinking differently. The facilitator explored thoughts and feelings of guilt again with Brian in the "pull-out" session. Brian was not experiencing the same level of intense feelings of guilt as he was earlier in the group and his thinking about his role in his sister's death had also started to shift. Brian was able to state that he wished he had picked up the screws and he wished his Dad, who was outside with him, had picked up the screws too, but his Dad thought he had picked them up. He said that a lot of times he does not do what he is asked to do right away. For the first time he said that his sister's death was an "accident," and he did not seem to hold himself as accountable for her death as he did in the beginning of the group meetings.

3. What do I do when children avoid talking about the trauma and loss?

It is common for children to try to avoid talking about what happened. They may be scared that if they talk about what happened they will start to cry and fall apart, or become more symptomatic and feel really scared or sad again. Avoidance is one of the hallmark responses of posttraumatic stress symptoms. So that the clinician is not colluding with the child in avoiding talking about it, session 2 briefly introduces the topic of what happened. However, at this point it is very important to allow the child to decide what she or he wants to share or is comfortable sharing. At this point the facilitator should not probe further as the child may not have the coping skills to talk about what happened and we want to avoid having the child becoming overwhelmed. However, session 2 will give the clinician an idea of the level of avoidance and if the child is struggling more with traumatic distress, separation distress, or both. The Clinical Chart also provides the clinician with a constant reminder of what event(s) bothers the child the most, is the saddest for the child, and what is the hardest to talk about. If the child does not share about any of these topics in session 2, it is an indication that as the child proceeds through the intervention, the clinician may need to be more directive. For example, if the child did not include any of the noted events from the assessment, then in session 6, after the child has learned coping skills, the clinician should ask the child which event he/she would like to focus on in the trauma narrative sessions. Or the clinician may even suggest the child begin with the event that the child noted was the hardest to talk about, and that the other events can also be reviewed in the "Another Important Story" worksheet.

In session 4 children should be provided education about feelings of avoidance and re-experiencing. Psychoeducation can provide normalization and lets the child know that these are common reactions for someone who has experienced a traumatic event. It lets the child know that "he/she is not going crazy." Having an open discussion about these feelings may also lead to some reduction in the level of avoidance and prepare the child for sharing more in the trauma narrative sessions about what happened.

Some children may draw, discuss, and have their story written but are scared to share their story with others. In these cases, clinicians can ask the child if he or she wants to share his or her story or if he/she wants the clinician to hold up the picture and read the story. Often children will allow the clinician to read the story and then, after some time, when the child feels more comfortable and has processed more of his or her trauma narrative, they will share and read the story.

Vignette: Session 4: avoidance behavior is addressed in the session

During session 4 when the other children were expressing their feelings related to Hurricane Katrina, Ava began to laugh inappropriately. The group members confronted Ava and asked her why she was laughing. Ava just stared at them and did not know what to say. The group facilitator quickly stated, "You know sometimes it is really hard to talk about your feelings. Sometimes when people have had really terrible things happen, they try not to think about it – they try to avoid it by doing different things such as wanting to talk about other things or sometimes by even joking around to change the topic. It is really important that we respect one another in here when someone shares his/her feelings." There was silence in the room for about 20 seconds with all of the children just sitting in their chairs. The group facilitator then said, "I wonder who would like to share more about his/her feelings related to Hurricane Katrina."

Ava, knowing that the facilitator was talking about her, was the first to talk. She disclosed that her family had not evacuated before the storm and that she had been at the New Orleans Convention Center in the days immediately following the hurricane. She recalled a soldier had a gun and was pointing it at her family and she also remembered that she heard that someone got shot. Ava was able to state that she felt "really, really scared." The group facilitator thanked her and praised her for telling her story to everyone and for sharing how scared she felt. After Ava finished, another child shared her Katrina experience and said to Ava that she felt "really scared too." She stated that at one point when she was in the flood waters, she thought she was going to drown.

The group facilitators normalized the children's feelings and discussed how sometimes these memories can bring back traumatic feelings almost like it is happening all over again. The facilitators explained that as they talk about what happened, share their feelings, and use their deep breathing exercises and other things that make them feel calm, the scary feelings won't feel so intense and the scary feelings will start to go away. The session ended with all of the children doing the deep breathing and stretching exercises. Ava finished the exercise by clapping her hands and singing a song that made the children laugh. Ava seemed pleased that she used her humor to make a difficult session end in a fun way.

Vignette: Sessions 7 and 10: Denise was scared to share her story

Denise, an 11-year-old sixth grader, completed her trauma narrative individually with one of the group facilitators during the "pull-out" session. She had procrastinated and did not complete her drawing in session 6 so she did not share it with the other group members. Denise's aunt died due to a drive-by shooting. During session 7, Denise was encouraged to share her drawings and stories with other group members. She stated, "I'm afraid to, I'm afraid I will start crying." Another fifth grader in the group, named Sasha, responded, "Remember, it's okay to cry, sometimes you have to let it out." Denise said, "I don't want to do it. It will make me too sad." One of the group facilitators said, "Your story is really important and we all want you to be heard. What would make it easier for you to share your story?" Denise asked the group leader to read her story and gave each one of her drawings to the other three members in the group to hold up while the group leader read through Denise's narrative. When the group leader was finished reading the story, everyone clapped and praised Denise for sharing her story.

Denise continued to learn and utilize healthy coping skills to manage emotional distress throughout the remainder of the group intervention. During session 10, the group members celebrated their progress and were very proud upon receiving their "My Story" book. Denise enthusiastically flipped through the pages of her book and she shouted, "I'm ready to read my story now!" Denise stood in front of her group members and read through her entire trauma narrative. Again, the other group members clapped and praised Denise for sharing her story.

4. What do I do when children ask questions about the violence or death that I cannot answer?

There are many questions that children may ask that we do not have the answers to. Or, our answers may be based on our own beliefs and not necessarily on the child's or family's beliefs. For example, what happens to someone after they die? Children often have many questions that they wonder about but have not had the opportunity to ask. Some of the questions lead children to continue to worry. It is important to provide a safe opportunity for children to express the questions that they have wanted to ask or have been struggling with by themselves. Clinicians can let children know that sometimes we do not have all of the answers to a question but that asking the question can help us feel better. Also, many questions are better answered by the child's family so that the discussion is provided within the cultural and spiritual context of the family. There are some questions that may be followed up with providing educational information. Session 4 provides the time for the child to explore questions, and also for the clinician to provide more information for certain topic areas if indicated, such as suicide, criminal trials, or disasters. If the clinician does not have this information readily available, he or she can provide the information in session 5 or in the individual "pull-out" session for specific children.

Vignette: Session 4: child asks important questions

Dominique, age 9, was receiving GTI for Children individually to address issues dealing with the murder of her sister, Tia (age 25), who was killed by her boyfriend, David, who then killed himself. Dominique spent a lot of time with her sister, who was her only sibling, and she used to call David her big brother. Dominique began GTI for Children about nine months after the murder-suicide.

In session 4, Dominique was reluctant to ask questions, stating that she did not have any questions. The therapist explained that sometimes children have questions about what happened, but that they never ask anyone because they are scared to ask. The therapist continued with the feelings education activity and told Dominique that she would leave the special questions worksheet out in case Dominique had any questions that she wanted to ask, either in this session or anytime they met together.

After they finished the feelings activity, the therapist asked again if there were any questions that she would like to write down and said that, if so, the therapist would write them for her. Dominique gave the therapist the worksheet that had "Questions" at the top and said, "Okay, you write them." Dominique then, without hesitation, began stating questions for the therapist to write down. She asked the following questions:

Why did he do it?
Why did God let this happen?
Why did she have to die?
Why can't she come back alive now?
Is God going to punish him?
What happened to him? Did he just go crazy or something?
Do you think she is a spirit?
Do you think I will ever see my sister again?
Where is heaven?
What if they were still alive?
Where did he shoot her?

After sharing her questions, the therapist praised Dominique for being so brave to ask these questions. Knowing that the family was very religious, the therapist let Dominique know that maybe someone in Dominique's family would be able to help her with these questions. The therapist acknowledged that she did not know the answers and asked Dominique who she thought could answer the questions. She said "my mama," but Dominique was not ready to ask her mother these questions.

The next week the therapist continued to practice relaxation with Dominique who developed her own guided imagery based on her safe place, which was her home. At the end of the session, the therapist asked Dominique if she had thought any more about talking with her mother and asking her questions. She said she would and they agreed that the therapist would be with her. The next week Dominique's mother was invited to join the session. The therapist had spoken with the mother about the questions prior to this meeting, to help her prepare. Her mother was surprised that Dominique had all of these questions because she stated that "Dominique never talks about it," but that she was glad she was talking. Although it was hard for Dominique's mother to talk with Dominique about these questions, she had wanted to talk with her, and she had wondered what she was thinking.

Dominique was able to ask her mother the questions. Her mother's responses were grounded in her religious beliefs and she reassured Dominique that her sister "would always be her big sister and that now she is in heaven watching over her and will help protect her." She continued to explain "that while we can't understand why God takes who he does, we trust God," and "that we all have our time to go home and it was her time to be with God." Her mother told her that "only the Lord knows what got into him," and that while she cannot understand it either,

"God will handle all things." Dominique listened and she did not ask any further questions. The therapist let Dominique and her mother know that Dominique may have even more questions that she wants to ask and that she could continue to ask questions anytime she wants to in the future, and her mother agreed. The therapist worked with Dominique to identify and share how she was feeling after talking about these questions and to practice her relaxation exercises.

5. What do I do when children continue to live in unsafe areas and/or do not feel safe?

While clinicians are encouraged to work on all levels within an ecological context to enhance the child's safety, there are children who participate in GTI for Children who continue to live in unsafe communities, unsafe schools, and unsafe homes. The first step is to make sure the child feels safe in the individual or group setting. Some approaches to creating a safe place may be: consistent empathetic responses; an atmosphere that promotes a sense of safety such as a clean, soothing color, private room; informing the child of what will be addressed in the session before the meeting starts; following the same structure every session; allowing the child to stop or pause if he/she becomes overwhelmed; and following rules that promote safety such as respecting one another and not talking to others outside of the session about what another child said. In session 5, a direct conversation about what safety means to the child occurs. It is important during this session that the child is encouraged to think about different safe places and people in the child's life. If the child continues to live in a violent community, it is important that the child can begin to feel a sense of safety even if this occurs in his/her immediate context such as with his/her parent, in his/her home, or in his/her room. If the child discloses that he/she does not feel safe at home because domestic violence is occurring, the clinician should contact the parent who signed the consent and see if the parent will come to the school or the clinician's office to meet. It is helpful at this point to consult with a domestic violence expert in terms of best ways to approach this topic with the parent. If the parent is the victim of domestic violence, he/she may not be able or ready to confront the violence at this time. It is important that the parent is provided with community resources such as hotlines, shelters, or advocacy centers that can help him/her. The clinician can also let the parent know that the clinician will work on a safety plan with the child, and that it is important that the plan is created and/or shared with the parent and child.

Vignette: Session 5: Melissa feels that nowhere is safe

During session 5, a group of six 11-year-olds were defining what safety meant to them. They discussed people and places that made them feel safe. One of the members, Melissa, announced to everyone with great certainty that "no *place* is safe and no *one* is really safe." She continued to explain to the group members that "a fire could happen when I'm home and I could be burned, I could be walking down the street and fall and break my bones, or it could be a normal day and a hurricane could come again." The group members listened to her but did not agree. One member quickly said, "These things could happen, but they don't happen every day." Another member said in a rather sarcastic tone, "Did you fall down today and break your bones?" The group members tried to help Melissa understand that while these things *could* happen, they do not happen on a daily basis. The clinician also helped Melissa to see that these thoughts were not helpful for her and were leading to her feeling more anxious. The clinicians discussed the importance of challenging the thoughts and using self-talk with more positive thoughts. Melissa was able to use the grief and trauma wheel to see how her thought that something bad was going to happen was leading to her having stomachaches and that when she changed the thought, her feelings, body reactions, and behavior would change. The group members continued to help Melissa realize what a sense of safety means. Later, Melissa was able to name a lot of places that felt calm and things she could do to make herself feel safe.

Vignette: Session 5: tension and bullying overrides the planned group session

During the post-session reviews, the group facilitators noted that there were two girls, Mary and Lina, who at times would make "dissing" comments toward one another (i.e., unsupportive remarks and comments that made fun of one another). The facilitators would continually redirect the girls and ask all group members how they could help make the group feel safe so that everyone felt respected. The group members would also remind each other of the rules that they had set such as "listen to each other," "be respectful," and "don't say mean things."

In session 5, the group members were drawing a picture of a dream. Lina drew a picture of herself at a dance contest that she won. Mary had seen Lina's picture as she was drawing it and she also drew a picture of girls at a dance contest. When the group facilitators began working with the girls to discuss the drawing and to help them write a story, it became apparent that the drawings were actually about a recent conflict between Lina and Mary. Lina had stated that her dream was that she was in a dance contest and she beat Mary. Mary, listening closely to Lina rather than finishing her drawing, held up her picture and announced to the other group members, "This is my dream when there was a dance contest and everyone was invited except Lina." The other girls in the group started to laugh and Lina then said, "Hey here is my picture when I beat Mary in the dance contest." Again, the other girls laughed. Clearly, the group was not on task, which was to discuss scary or comforting dreams about the person who died.

The conflict between the girls was preventing the group session from proceeding as intended. One of the group facilitators stood up and interrupted everyone from finishing the activity. The facilitators reminded the girls that everyone was in the group because they had something scary happen and the purpose of the group was to help them feel better. The facilitator asked, "How can we make this a safe group?" A girl named Odyssey looked at the facilitator and asked, "What do you mean a safe group? Use your real words, Ms. Linda," implying that the facilitator needed to be more direct about what was occurring in group with Lina and Mary disrespecting each other and the tension between them. Ms. Linda directly acknowledged the tension between Lina and Mary and asked them and the other group members how they could work it out so they could be respectful of each other and mindful of each other's feelings. The girls came up with the idea that they could do role plays such as where one girl did not make the cheerleading squad and felt left out, and how the other girls could help her feel better, or another role play in which one girl says something to hurt another girl's feelings and they make up. Lina and Mary agreed that this would be helpful, and the girls put on skits with themes of helping each other and being inclusive. Lina and Mary both participated. After the skits, Lina and Mary apologized to each other in front of the other girls and agreed that they would "be nice to each other" and not do or say things to hurt the other girl's feelings. The facilitators ended the group with the guided imagery exercise and let the girls know that next week they would try to start about 20 minutes early so that they could finish what they had started in the group that day.

7. What do I do when a child experiences another violent event or death of someone close while participating in GTI for Children?

When children are living in areas where violence continues, they may be exposed to another violent event. In these cases it is very important to encourage the use of coping skills and to help the child find ways to relax his or her mind and body. Relaxation exercises should be practiced in every session as well as outside of the session. Also, the clinician may need to move the session 5 safety activity earlier in the model, or review it again if this has already been covered. If a child has another person close to him/her die, the clinician may include this loss as the child processes the primary loss that was identified in the pre-assessment. The child will decide which one he/she wants to focus on in the meetings, or may choose to focus on both. In the restorative questions the clinician may focus on themes that would pertain to both losses.

Vignette: Sessions 4 and 9: another person dies and Brenda is supported by the group

During session 4, the group members discussed spirituality as a source of strength when grieving the death of a loved one. Brenda, a 12-year-old sixth grader, asked, "Sometimes I get mad, why did God have to take my aunt away from me?" Denise responded, "God wanted her by Him and now she can watch over you." Brenda looked up and smiled. The group facilitator asked Brenda what her thoughts were with regard to Denise's response. Brenda said, "It makes me feel better that my aunt is watching over me." It was evident that Denise's response was comforting for Brenda.

By session 9, the group cohesion was strong. At the beginning of the session, Brenda stated that her uncle died of cancer the previous night. The group facilitators asked Brenda about her thoughts and feelings. Brenda replied, "My family is coming from Starkville today and everyone's going to be really sad and crying. I'm going by my Grandma's house because my Momma said 'I don't want her by that, she's already been through enough.' I'm trying not to cry in front of anyone because I don't want to make them upset." Sasha responded, "It's okay to cry. Sometimes it's not good to keep it all inside." One of the group facilitators asked, "Who do you have that you can talk to about your uncle and that you feel comfortable with if you do start to cry?" Brenda reported that she felt comfortable talking to her grandmother. Sherry, a 10-year-old fifth grader, said, "You can talk to us, everyone in the group." The other group members agreed that Brenda could talk with them about her uncle's death. Brenda spent the rest of the session drawing, writing, and discussing all of the things she liked about her life. Helping her to focus on the positive things in her life helped to balance her profound sadness.

8. What about having commemorative rituals or having parents attend the last meeting?

GTI for Children used to include a component in which group members were encouraged to bring special reminders or things that they cherished from their loved one who died. The group facilitators would try different approaches to remind the children to bring in something. However, often children would forget to bring something in, not want to or not have something to bring, or a child's parent would not want them to bring the special item or photograph to school. The children who did not bring in an item would then feel left out when the other group members shared. Therefore, this was eventually taken out of the model. However, if it seems appropriate and that it would work with a specific group of children, this type of activity can be very powerful to help children retain positive memories of the deceased and to become less scared talking about the person who died. When meeting individually with the child, the clinician can encourage the child to bring in a special item or photograph of the person who died, and if the child forgets, he or she may bring it in the following session. They can also problem-solve about ways to help the child remember, such as writing a reminder note in a special place or even calling the parent and asking the parent to help the child remember.

If GTI for Children is being conducted in a setting where the parents/caregivers are not available, such as at school, some clinicians have tried to invite the parents/caregivers to the last session so that the children can share what they have been doing in the intervention. However, past experience has been that some parents/caregivers attend and others are not able to, due to work demands or other scheduled events. It is often a real let-down for the children whose parents/caregivers do not attend and having a proxy stand in for the parent, such as a teacher, is not the same. Therefore, we do not recommend inviting the parents/caregivers to attend. If GTI for Children is provided in a hospital or group home where parents/caregivers are not available, it may be appropriate to have caring adults such as nurses or group home counselors come to the last session to serve as witnesses to the children's experiences and to show support. In some cases, an additional scheduled family meeting might be held at the end where the child can share with the parent/caregiver his or her "My Story" book. Data from our two follow-up studies suggest that when children ended GTI for Children and completed session 10, where the caring adult to share the book with was identified, the vast majority of the children had caring adults sign their book and the children shared the book with several caring adults.

If GTI for Children is being provided in a setting where the parents/caregivers are in attendance during the time the children are attending sessions, such as at a community mental health center or a bereavement center, the parents/caregivers could be invited into the meeting at the end of each session, whether GTI for Children was provided individually or in a group setting, and the children could share with their parents the work they did in their "My Story" book. Also, if the parents/caregivers have been through a similar traumatic event — if for example they were also exposed to the violent event or disaster or had someone close die — a simultaneous group for adults could take place while the children were participating in GTI for Children. Restorative Retelling (see www.vdbs.org for the manual for Restorative Retelling for adults, by E. K. Rynearson), which is very similar to GTI for Children, may be provided (Rynearson & Salloum, 2011). There are other treatments for adults such as the Complicated Grief Treatment (see www.complicatedgrief.org/bereavement for more information).

Vignette: Sessions 9–10: termination session becomes a commemoration for lost loved ones

While planning the termination celebration in session 9, a group of sixth graders, all of whom were in the group because of the death of someone close, came up on their own with the idea of each bringing in something in memory of the person who had died. Each child came to session 10 with something that reminded him/her of his/her loved one, such as pictures, memorial tee-shirts, and a necklace. Roland, who had been somewhat avoidant from the first session and who had taken on the role several times of the "group clown," stated on several occasions that he didn't want to share because he didn't want to cry. Roland brought in a 10-minute DVD with music and pictures of his grandmother that was played at her wake. He wore sunglasses because he didn't want the group members to see him cry. Another boy told him, "Sometimes crying can be a good thing. It helps you to get your feelings out," and all of the other members agreed. Roland eventually took off his sunglasses and let the other members see that his eyes were watery and filled with tears. The group members were very supportive toward Roland. The members asked him questions about his grandmother and Roland seemed to feel really proud to share his stories about his grandmother with the members.

REFERENCES

Rynearson, E. K. & Salloum, A. (2011). Restorative retelling: Revising the narrative of violent death. In R. Neimeyer & G. Thornton (Eds.), *Grief and bereavement in contemporary society: Bridging research and practice* (pp. 177–188). New York: Routledge.

Chapter 8

In-Session Guidance

This chapter provides one-page outlines of each session that can be used as quick reference guides for facilitating the sessions. Also, if there are co-facilitators implementing GTI for Children, they can use these outlines to decide who will be the lead for each activity. Previous facilitators of GTI for Children have reported that these session-by-session outlines have been helpful implementation tools.

SESSION AGENDAS

These agendas can be used during each session as guides. Clinicians should read the full description of the session in Chapter 6 prior to facilitating the session. Also, it is helpful to bring each session outline into the meeting with the child(ren) as a reminder of topics to cover. Group facilitators should review these agendas before each session, and if there are two facilitators, plan the sections that each facilitator will lead and co-lead. Also, clinicians should note on the outline if a topic is not discussed in a specific session so that it can be included in the following or another session.

SESSION 1

1. *Purpose and introduction:*

   a. Welcome.
   b. Introduce facilitators and have children introduce themselves.
   c. Name tags.
   d. Light snack.
   e. Explain what they will be doing in the session for that day.
   f. Explain schedule.
   g. Explain purpose of group.

2. *Rules:*

   a. Have every child state at least one rule.
   b. Explain confidentiality.

3. *Increase comfort level*:

   a. Conduct an ice breaker.

4. *Reason for participating:*

   a. Have each member briefly state why he or she is in the group or meeting individually.

5. *Anger management and relaxation:*

   a. Explain that sometimes after something terrible happens, some children and adults may feel angry.
   b. Ask for reasons why they may feel angry.
   c. Complete "My Anger Signs" worksheet.
   d. Let them know that during this group, or in individual meetings, they will be working on ways to manage anger and the first step is learning about anger signs that occur in our bodies.
   e. Identify and act out anger signs.
   f. Teach deep breathing exercises.

6. *Supportive adults:*

   a. Have each child think about who this might be for them and write down their names and who they are in relationship to the child.
   b. Encourage them to talk with this person about what they are doing in the group.

7. *Enjoyment / activities*:

   a. What does the child enjoy?
   b. How can they get involved and/or do activities they enjoy?

Ending and announcements: Ask the group for ideas about a way to close today's session. If they cannot agree on one idea, discuss this next time. Remind them about confidentiality.

SESSION 2

Introduction:

    a. Welcome the children.
    b. Offer a light snack.
    c. Explain today's agenda.

1. *Goals:*

    a. Review the goals with everyone and have them sign that they understand the goals (see "Goals" worksheet).

2. *Grief and trauma education:*

    a. Provide education about grief and trauma reactions.

3. *First storytelling exercise:*

    a. Explain special book entitled "My Story."
    b. Allow child to choose one worksheet: "A Scary Thing Happened," "I Really Miss," or "When I think about _____, I think . . ."
    c. Complete narrative activities (draw, discuss, write, and witness).

4. *Anger management / relaxation:*

    a. Anger signs: ask if children noticed any of their anger signs this past week.
    b. Explore ways to cool down.
    c. Explain rewards (stickers or pencils) for practicing.

Ending and announcements: End with the deep breathing exercise and a group closing ritual, if the group has developed one. Make sure the children know how many more times they will meet.

SESSION 3

Introduction:

    a. Welcome the children.
    b. Offer a light snack.
    c. Explain today's agenda.

1. *Briefly review last session:*

    a. Review last week's topic of grief and traumatic reactions.
    b. Ask if the children can remember a time when they felt angry this past week. Did they notice their anger sign? Did they try one of the ways to calm or cool down? Give a sticker or pencil as a reward and encourage them to continue to use these techniques.
    c. Explore possible ways the child might react to real-life situations that make him or her feel angry.

2. *Family support activity / changes:*

    a. Discuss how changes sometimes occur after a loss or trauma.
    b. Allow child to choose between "My Family" and "Changes I Have Noticed" worksheets.
    c. Complete narrative activities (draw, discuss, write, and witness).

3. *Anniversaries / holidays:*

    a. Discuss ways of coping.

4. *Spirituality / beliefs:*

    a. Discuss spirituality and beliefs.
    b. Allow child to choose between "My Prayer," "My Poem," and "My Song" worksheets.
    c. Complete narrative activities (draw, discuss, write, and witness).

Ending and announcements: End with the deep breathing exercise and a group closing ritual, if the group has developed one. Make sure the children know how many more times they will meet.

SESSION 4

Introduction:

a. Welcome the children.
b. Offer a light snack.
c. Explain what they will be doing in the group during this session.
d. Briefly review last session.
e. Ask if children practiced the relaxation exercise or were able to recognize anger signs or use cool down strategies. Give a sticker or pencil as a reward and encourage them to continue to use these techniques.

1. *Feelings:*

a. Address feelings: scared, angry, sad, worried, guilty, brave, confused, and happy.
b. Explain common traumatic responses such as avoidance (not wanting to be reminded) and re-experiencing (intrusive thoughts and images etc.).
c. Complete narrative activities (draw, discuss, write, and witness) with the "My Feelings" worksheet.
d. Teach strategies for coping with re-experiencing the traumatic event. Continue education of grief and traumatic feeling reactions.

2. *Questions:*

a. Allow time for questions. See "Questions" worksheet.
b. Provide specific educational information about traumatic event, if needed.
c. If time allows, have child express "I wish" thoughts and complete narrative activities (draw, discuss, write, and witness) with the worksheet.

Ending and announcements: End with the deep breathing exercise and a group closing ritual, if the group has developed one. Remind children to identify anger signs, and practice cool down strategies including relaxation. Make sure the children know how many more times they will meet.

SESSION 5

Introduction:

    a. Welcome the children.
    b. Offer a light snack.
    c. Explain what they will be doing in the group during this session.
    d. Briefly review last session.
    e. Ask if children practiced the relaxation exercise or were able to recognize anger signs or use cool down strategies. Give rewards and encourage them to continue to use these techniques.

1. *Dreams*:

    a. Discuss types of dreams: comforting and scary.
    b. Complete narrative activities (draw, discuss, write, and witness) with the "My Dream" worksheet.
    c. Read suggested book or do a comforting activity to help with scary dreams.

2. *Safety:*

    a. Ask the children if they know what "feeling safe" means. Help each child define feeling safe.
    b. Let the child choose one of the three worksheets.
    c. Complete narrative activities (draw, discuss, write, and witness) with either "My Safe Place," "My Safe Person," or "My Protective Shield" worksheet.
    d. Guided imagery: begin with deep breathing exercise and facilitate guided imagery about feeling safe.

Ending and announcements: Inform the children in the group that after the next session the clinician will meet individually with them. End with the deep breathing exercise and a group closing ritual, if the group has developed one. Remind children to identify anger signs and practice cool down strategies including relaxation. Make sure the children know how many more times they will meet.

SESSION 6

(Read instructions for session 6, "pull-out," and session 7.)

Introduction:

  a. Welcome the children.
  b. Offer a light snack.
  c. Explain what they will be doing in the group during this session.
  d. Briefly review last session.
  e. Ask if children practiced relaxation exercise or were able to recognize anger signs or use cool down strategies. Give rewards and encourage them to continue to use these techniques.

1. *Coherent narrative (see manual for instructions):*

  a. Begin story of what happened.
  b. Complete narrative activities (draw, discuss, write, and witness).
  c. Listen for signs of *bravery and hope* and highlight these instances.
  d. Consider using "Another Important Story" worksheet.

Ending and announcements: To help moderate any distress, this session should end with the relaxation exercise and the children should be encouraged to practice it every day during the week. A reward of stickers or pencils may be offered next session for practicing. Inform the children in the group that one of the clinicians will meet individually with them.

INDIVIDUAL "PULL-OUT" SESSION

1. If the child was absent during any of the first six sessions, address the topic(s) that were not covered.
2. Review story of what happened.
3a. Complete narrative activities (draw, discuss, write, and witness) with "My Worst Moment" worksheet.
3b. Worst moment drawing.
4. Address the child's feelings of guilt.
5. Explore if the child is exposed to trauma reminders. If so, discuss coping strategies.
6. Reinforce use of relaxation. Practice individually with the child.
7. Address any unique needs of the child.

SESSION 7

Introduction:

    a. Welcome the children.
    b. Offer a light snack.
    c. Explain what they will be doing in the group during this session.
    d. Briefly review last session.
    e. Ask if children practiced relaxation exercise or were able to recognize anger signs or use cool down strategies. Give rewards and encourage them to continue to use these techniques.

1. *Complete what happened narrative*:

    a. Spend time on completing the activities from session 6 so that a complete narrative has been created, explored, and shared.

2. *Coping and supports:*

    a. List multiple ways of coping or feeling better. Complete "Things I Can Do to Feel Better" worksheet.
    b. During this activity, predict re-occurrences of distress and encourage use of new skills of coping.
    c. Spend time completing a creative art activity that highlights the child's coping list.

Ending and announcements: End with the deep breathing exercise and remind them to practice cooling down when they feel anger signs. If a closing ritual was developed, end with the ritual. Remind group members about confidentiality. Let them know how many meetings are remaining.

115

SESSION 8

Introduction:

    a. Welcome the children.
    b. Offer a light snack.
    c. Explain what they will be doing in the group during this session.
    d. Briefly review last session. Return "cool" typed or perhaps framed copy of the child's coping list.
    e. Ask if children practiced relaxation exercise or were able to recognize anger signs or use cool down strategies. Give rewards and encourage them to continue to use these techniques.

1. *Memories:*

    a. Let the child choose one of the four worksheets.
    b. Complete narrative activities (draw, discuss, write, and witness) with either "My Favorite Memory," "The Thing I Miss the Most," "A Happy Time Together" or "My Story About _____."

2. *Meaning:*

    a. Explore meaning of loss(es).
    b. Explore any ambivalent feelings toward the deceased or loss.

Start discussing and planning for ending celebration

Ending and announcements: End with the deep breathing exercise and remind them to practice cooling down when they feel anger signs. If a closing ritual was developed, end with the ritual. Remind group members about confidentiality. Let them know how many meetings are remaining.

SESSION 9

Introduction:

- a. Welcome the children.
- b. Offer a light snack.
- c. Explain what they will be doing in the group during this session.
- d. Briefly review last session.
- e. Ask if children practiced relaxation exercise or used any of the things on their list of things to feel better. Give rewards and encourage them to continue to use these techniques.

1. *Positive comforting memories:*

- a. Additional time for children to talk about their loss(es) and share their experiences.
- b. Children may want to complete the other worksheets from session 8.

If time allows, provide time for children to make sure all worksheets that were previously worked on have been completed.

2. *Focus on the positive:*

- a. Complete narrative activities (draw, discuss, write, and witness) with either "My Hope for the Future" or "Things about My Life I Like" worksheet.
- b. When the child is discussing his or her drawing, the clinician should ask exploratory questions to elicit positive visions of the future or positive aspects of the child's current situation.

NOTE

If the child needs more time completing the memories worksheet, these two worksheets may be completed in session 10.

3. *Ending:*

- a. Discuss that there will be one more meeting of the group after this session, or that children being seen individually will only meet one more time.
- b. Plan celebration and type of food (note any allergies that children have to specific foods).
- c. Lead a discussion about how hard it may be for some children to end GTI for Children and about the feelings of sadness or anger that may surface, but also discuss the positive benefits of attending the sessions and their new skills of coping with sadness, fear, anger, and other feelings.

4. *Goal review:*

    a. Complete goal review. This may also be completed during an individual post-evaluation meeting after session 10.

Ending and announcements: End with the deep breathing exercise and remind them to practice cooling down when they feel anger signs. If a closing ritual was developed, end with the ritual. Remind group members about confidentiality. Remind the children again that there is one more meeting.

SESSION 10

Introduction:

    a. Welcome the children.
    b. Explain what they will be doing in the group during this session.
    c. Wait to eat and enjoy the food until after the last drawing exercise is completed.

1. *Reconnecting:*

    a. Read aloud the last worksheet and explain that the book is not complete until the child has shared it with a caring adult. Have the child identify the adult who will review and sign the book.
    b. Make sure that all children have some type of activity or outlet that provides them a "break" from the stress and grief. If not, work with the child and parent to find activities that may help the child.

2. *Review, celebrate, and say goodbye:*

    a. Enjoy food.
    b. Present certificates.
    c. Present "My Story" book.
    d. Encourage child to share book with primary caregiver and/or caring adult.
    e. Let them know you will be contacting their parents/caregivers.

Chapter 9

Treatment Adherence

This chapter provides an adherence checklist as one way to monitor treatment fidelity. A six-step process is encouraged to help the facilitator balance between adhering to the treatment model and meeting the unique needs of the child.

ADHERENCE TO GTI FOR CHILDREN

Treatment adherence checklists are designed to help clinicians monitor treatment implementation so that the model is delivered as it is intended to be delivered. The checklists are used to monitor what has been provided when, and they may also be used to identify if there are any problems in the delivery. Checklists are one method of treatment fidelity but it may not be the most accurate since it is a clinician self-report and does not capture the skill of the clinician providing the information, the level of sophistication in terms of how the information was provided, or the level of therapeutic alliance. For example, using the current checklist, the clinician indicates if the material was "sufficiently" covered. Sufficient coverage can be subjective and the clinician, client, and third parties may all have a different opinion about what is sufficient. Other methods of treatment fidelity include consistent supervision by a trained GTI for Children clinician and/or independent ratings based on audio- or video-taped sessions. Nonetheless, for purpose of tracking that the essential content is covered, clinicians are encouraged to complete the adherence checklist and to use clinical judgment to determine if the information covered was sufficient.

Although the ordering of intervention topics is specified according to theory, in some cases the sequence may need to be changed in order to meet the child's immediate needs. Remember, when a session is missed, follow the procedures for missed sessions. There have been some occasions where a parent/caregiver provides parental consent for his or her child to participate in GTI for Children, and then is not available for a parent meeting. In these cases, try to meet the parent/caregiver at flexible times, if possible, such as in the evening or at weekends. If this is not possible, try to schedule a phone meeting. In cases where the parent/caregiver meeting has not occurred but the parent wanted his or her child to receive GTI for Children, we have provided GTI for Children to the child and then tried to schedule a meeting or phone call at the end to discuss the child's progress.

Clinicians, whether conducting GTI for Children as a group or individually with a child, are encouraged to engage in the following activities which will increase adherence:

1. Read over the session instructions (see Chapter 6) prior to session facilitation.
2. Schedule a pre-session meeting to prepare for facilitation (see Pre-Session Review, Chapter 3).
3. Review the agenda before each session (see Chapter 8) and use it to guide the session.
4. After each session, complete the adherence checklist (see Chapter 9).
5. After each group session, review the post-session review (see Post-Session Review, Chapter 3).
6. Seek clinical supervision as needed.

ADHERENCE CHECKLIST

Name of Clinician: _____

Circle: Individual or Group

If group: Where: _____ When: _____

Co-Leader: _____

If individual: Initials of child: _____

Instructions: One adherence checklist is to be completed for each child after the child participates in each session. After every session the clinician should review the adherence checklist.

    Since GTI for Children is to be used in a flexible manner depending on the child's needs, an item on the adherence checklist may not have been covered during the scheduled session. Therefore, whenever the item is covered, regardless of the order, the clinician should write the session number in the box when that item was covered. It is important to complete this adherence checklist immediately after each session is completed.

    Other topics that are not described in the intervention and that emerge should be noted in the comments section. Having this type of documentation is not only important for ensuring adherence to the GTI for Children model, but it can also be used as a systematic way of learning about patterns of other common issues – it may be that the topics identified and documented in the comments section are important for various populations being served.

Meeting Individually with Parent or Caregiver:

Date: _____

Check the box if the item was sufficiently covered in the parent meeting.

❏ Explained purpose of intervention.

❏ Provided education about grief and trauma.

❏ Discussed ways that parents can help children.

❏ Discussed open communication.

❏ Taught relaxation to parent for child to practice.

Comments:

_____

_____

_____

GTI FOR CHILDREN ADHERENCE CHECKLIST: CHILD COMPONENTS

Write the session number when that topic was covered in the box.

Session 1: Date: _____

- ☐ Child briefly stated reason for participation.
- ☐ Set rules – reviewed confidentiality.
- ☐ Began anger management – identified anger signs.
- ☐ Taught relaxation exercise.
- ☐ Identified supportive adults.
- ☐ Identified activities child enjoys.

Comments:

_____

_____

_____

Session 2: Date: _____

- ☐ Provided education about grief and traumatic stress.
- ☐ Child chose and completed first story activity.
- ☐ Taught anger management.
- ☐ Practiced relaxation.

Comments:

_____

_____

_____

Session 3: Date: _____

- ☐ Addressed anger management skills.
- ☐ Discussed family supports and changes.
- ☐ Discussed anniversaries and ways of coping.
- ☐ Discussed spirituality/beliefs.
- ☐ Practiced relaxation.

Comments:

_____

_____

_____

Session 4: Date: _____

- ☐ Discussed common feelings after something terrible happens.
- ☐ Explained avoidance and re-experiencing.
- ☐ Allowed child to ask questions.
- ☐ Practiced relaxation.

Comments:

_____

_____

_____

Session 5: Date: _____

- ☐ Explored dreams.
- ☐ Discussed definition of safety.
- ☐ Child drew safe place or safe person.
- ☐ Practiced relaxation exercise (deep breathing and/or guided imagery).

Comments:

_____

_____

_____

Session 6: Date: _____

- ☐ Helped child draw and/or discuss story about what happened.
- ☐ Highlighted signs of bravery and hope.
- ☐ Practiced relaxation.

Comments:

_____

_____

_____

Individual "pull-out" session: Date: _____

- ☐ Reviewed story about what happened.
- ☐ Identified worst moment.
- ☐ Listened for and corrected distortions.
- ☐ Identified trauma reminders and ways to cope with these reminders.
- ☐ Inquired directly about feelings of guilt.
- ☐ Practiced relaxation.

Comments:

_____

_____

_____

Session 7: Date: _____

- ❑ Completed narrative.
- ❑ Discussed ways of coping.
- ❑ Identified supportive people.
- ❑ Practiced relaxation.

Comments:

_____

_____

_____

Session 8: Date: _____

- ❑ Discussed memories.
- ❑ Practiced relaxation.

Comments:

_____

_____

_____

Session 9: Date: _____

- ❑ Discussed positive memories.
- ❑ Discussed positive aspects of current situation and positive vision of future (may be completed in session 10).
- ❑ Discussed ending.
- ❑ Practiced relaxation.

Comments:

_____

_____

_____

Session 10: Date: _____

- ☐ Reviewed and celebrated progress.
- ☐ Said goodbye.

Comments:

_____

_____

_____

GTI FOR CHILDREN ADHERENCE PERCENTAGE

Parent meeting:

Total topics discussed _____ of 5 = _____%

Child meetings:

Total topics discussed _____ of 44 = _____%

Total topics _____ of 49 = _____%

SUMMARY OF GTI FOR CHILDREN MEETINGS

Total number of **group** sessions attended: _____

Total number of **individual** sessions attended: _____ (include the "pull-out" session)

Total number of times met with child (add group + individual): _____

Total number of sessions **missed**: _____

Reasons for missed sessions:

_____ Child was not at school (do not know why)

_____ School schedule (field trip, activity, half day, etc.)

_____ Child was suspended or expelled for fighting or other reason.

Explain: _____

_____ Child was at school and did not want to attend because _____

_____ Transportation problems (clinic-based GTI for Children)

_____ Parent had scheduling difficulty (clinic-based GTI for Children)

_____ Parent forgot meeting (clinic-based GTI for Children)

_____ Other. Explain: _____

ADDITIONAL MEETINGS BEYOND THE GTI FOR CHILDREN SESSIONS

Enter the number of additional meetings that occurred beyond the GTI for Children model. If there were no additional meetings enter 0.

1. How many additional meetings occurred with the parent (do not include the one scheduled meeting)? _____

Explain reason and content of the parent meeting(s):

_____

_____

_____

2. How many additional individual child sessions occurred? _____

Explain reason and content of the individual session(s):

_____

_____

_____

3. How many additional group sessions occurred? _____

Explain reason and content of the group session(s):

_____

_____

_____

4. How may family meetings occurred? _____

Explain reason and content of the family session(s):

_____

_____

_____

Total number of meetings beyond the described GTI for Children sessions: _____

GTI for Children Activity Sheets

The appendix provides activity sheets that correspond with each GTI for Children session. The session number for when the handout or activity sheet is to be used is at the bottom of each page so that facilitators can easily prepare for the sessions. Also, all of the activity sheets are in one appendix so that they can be easily located and copied.

MY STORY ACTIVITY SHEETS

The following worksheets accompany GTI for Children. The first worksheet entitled "My Story" includes lines for writing and is to be copied and used with all DDWW activities. It is to be used to record the child's story. Usually after the restorative discussion the child tells his or her story and the facilitator writes the story for the child. Older children may want to write the story by themselves, but for younger children, having the facilitator write the story allows the child to focus on telling the story, rather than the focus being on writing neatly and spelling correctly.

Some sessions provide a few worksheets so that the child can choose the ones that he or she wants to complete. If time allows, children can complete more than one.

The evaluation form for the goals is also included. We recommend that this evaluation is included as part of the post-assessment evaluation (see Chapter 4 for a discussion about pre- and post-assessment).

WORKSHEETS BY SESSIONS

First page: "My Story" used to record all written narratives. Copy this page so that blank sheets can be used throughout the intervention.

Session 1:   Title page
My Anger Signs
My Support People
Relaxation handout (given to child and parent)

Session 2:   Goals
                    Grief and Trauma Wheel
                    Choose one: A Scary Thing Happened, I Really Miss *or* When I Think About
                    _____ I Think
                    Things I Can Do To Cool Myself When I Am Angry

Session 3:   *Choose one:* My Family *or* Changes I Have Noticed
                    Choose one: My Prayer, My Poem *or* My Song

Session 4:   My Feelings
                    My Questions
                    I Wish (if time allows)

Session 5:   My Dream
                    Choose one: My Safe Place, My Safe Person *or* My Protective Shield
                    Safe Place Guided Imagery (for clinicians to use)

Sessions 6, "Pull-Out," and 7:

These worksheets are completed during session 6, the "pull-out" session, and session 7. There
are three different worksheet series that can be used. Choose one for the child. If the child is
experiencing traumatic stress primarily due to a disaster, use the first set. If the child is experiencing traumatic stress primarily due to violence or having someone close die or any other type
of loss, use the second set. If the child experiences frustration from drawing and/or if time is
limited, choose the third option and spend more time on discussion and writing.

Set one: Before The Disaster, During The Disaster, After The Disaster

Set two: Before It Happened, When It Happened, After It Happened

Third option: My Story About What Happened

Pull-out session: My Worst Moment

Session 6 or 7:   Another Important Story (optional)

Session 7:   Things I Can Do To Feel Better
                    (include separate art project)

Session 8:   *Choose one:* My Favorite Memory, The Thing I Miss The
                    Most, A Happy Time Together, My Story About _____

Session 9:   My Hope For The Future
                    Things About My Life That I Like

Session 10:   Congratulations!

Evaluation: Review of Goals

My Story

_____
_____
_____
_____
_____
_____
_____
_____
_____
_____
_____
_____
_____
_____
_____
_____
_____
_____
_____
_____
_____
_____
_____
_____
_____
_____
_____

My Story

By

_____

My Anger Signs

What are your anger signs?

❑ Mad face ❑ Tighten fist

❑ Feel hot ❑ Heart races

❑ Clench teeth ❑ Chest goes out with arms back

Other signs:

_____

_____

_____

I feel angry when

_____

_____

_____

One thing that still makes me feel angry is

_____

_____

_____

My Support People

THE RELAXING TWO STEP EXERCISE (BY ALISON SALLOUM, PH.D.)

This simple relaxation exercise is for young children. All of the steps are in twos so that they can remember how to complete it. When teaching this exercise, the instructor should do it with the child so that he or she understands the steps. Have the children practice this with their caregivers and on their own. After the child has mastered this exercise he or she may want to make up a "Fun Two Step Exercise" with fun moves as a way to be silly and interact with the teaching adult.

Step 1: Breathing (practice the breathing step over and over and encourage the child to do at least this step every day)

Breathe in slowly through your nose (in for two, hold for two, blow out for two)
Breathe in slowly through your nose (in for two, hold for two, blow out for two)

Step 2: Stretching

Stretch up (reach for the stars) and relax
Stretch up (reach for the stars) and relax

Step 3: Muscle Relaxation (older children may want to include other muscles such as leg muscles)

Tighten your arm muscles (tighten, tighten your big muscles and hold for two) and let them fall like noodles

Tighten your arm muscles (tighten, tighten your big muscles and hold for two) and let them fall like noodles

Step 4: Cognitive Thought (say)

I feel relaxed
I feel relaxed

Repeat Step 1

GOALS

The purpose of this program is for you to be able to express your grief and loss and for you to feel better by making any traumatic reactions go away or not happen as much.

    Below are three of the main goals:

1. To learn more about grief and trauma reactions.
2. To express my thoughts and feelings about what happened.
3. To learn ways to calm myself down.

The counselor will work with you to reach these goals. Please sign below. Signing means that you have read the goals above and understand the purpose of this program.

_____   _____

Sign your name   Date

_____   _____

Counselor   Date

GRIEF AND TRAUMA WHEEL

<table>
<tr><td colspan="2">Thoughts</td><td colspan="2">Feelings</td></tr>
<tr><td><u>Grief</u></td><td><u>Trauma</u></td><td><u>Grief</u></td><td><u>Trauma</u></td></tr>
<tr><td>Missing a person</td><td>Can't stop thinking about how the person died</td><td>Sad</td><td>Intense anger</td></tr>
</table>

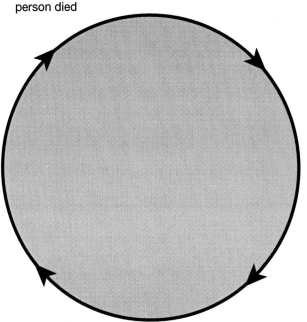

<table>
<tr><td colspan="2">Behaviors</td><td colspan="2">Body Reactions</td></tr>
<tr><td><u>Grief</u></td><td><u>Trauma</u></td><td><u>Grief</u></td><td><u>Trauma</u></td></tr>
<tr><td>Crying</td><td>Angry outbursts
Temper tantrums
Fighting</td><td>Headaches
Stomachaches</td><td>Heart racing
Feeling like traumatic moment is happening again</td></tr>
</table>

A Scary Thing Happened

I Really Miss

When I Think About

_____

_____

_____

I Think . . .

Things I Can Do To Cool Myself When I Am Angry

My Family

Changes I
Have Noticed

My Prayer

My Poem

My Song

My Feelings

My Questions

I Wish

My Dream

My Safe Place

My Safe Person

My Protective Shield

SAFE PLACE GUIDED IMAGERY (FOR CLINICIANS TO USE)

If you want close your eyes . . .

Take a few minutes and settle yourself down. Let your body relax, relax your arms, relax your legs, relax your shoulders, relax the muscles in your face. As you start to relax, take a deep breath in and breathe out your stress, take a deep breath in and breathe out your stress (remember to breathe in through your nose and out through your mouth, filling up your stomach each time).

You are going to take a guided walk to your special place or to see your special person that makes you feel safe. This is the place where you feel safe, where everything is okay, where you feel protected, guarded, watched over and cared for [add child's definition of feeling safe].

Go ahead and, in your mind, walk there and when you get there, stop. Look around, see how nice everything looks.

What do you see?

What do you hear?

Notice how good you feel.

Notice how safe you feel.

Since you can only stay for a minute take a deep breath in and let these safe feelings come inside you.

Feel how nice it is to feel relaxed and safe.

Tell yourself that you can come back here in the future, and you will be back, but for now, you will take the safe feelings with you. Go ahead in your mind, walk away. As you walk, take a deep breath in and breathe out, and when you are ready, count from 5 backwards and open your eyes and return . . . 5, 4, 3, 2, and 1.

Alison Salloum

Before The Disaster

During The Disaster

After The Disaster

Before It Happened

When It Happened

After It Happened

My Story About What Happened

My Worst Moment

pull-out

Another Important Story

Things I Can Do To Feel Better

My Favorite Memory

The Thing
I Miss The
Most

A Happy Time Together

My Story About

_____

My Hope For The Future

Things About My Life That I Like

CONGRATULATIONS!

This is the end of my very special book, but I know that I can look at it anytime I want to and remember all the special things that we did in counseling.

I have been very brave and talked about scary things and things that made me sad.

I have learned how to calm myself down and I have learned different ways of dealing with stress so that I can feel better.

A special adult cares about me. I can talk to this adult about my thoughts and feelings, and I would like to share this book with him or her.

As a way of ending this book, I will share this book with my special adult whose name is

_____.

Once we have talked about all that I have done in this book, we will both sign our names as a way of knowing I am a brave, strong person.

My caring, safe person:

_____
Signature

My name:

_____
Signature

© 2015, *Grief and Trauma in Children: An Evidence-Based Treatment Manual*, Alison Salloum, Routledge.

REVIEW OF GOALS

Rating Sheet

For each statement, say how much you learned, expressed yourself, and how helpful the counseling was for you.

HOW MUCH?

None	A Little	Some	A Lot	A Whole Lot
0	1	2	3	4

GRIEF AND TRAUMA INTERVENTION FOR CHILDREN

Review of Goals

These goals were set at the beginning of counseling. On the scales, please CIRCLE a number that shows how much you learned, expressed yourself, and how helpful the counseling was for you. Read each sentence aloud and read all the responses each time.

How much?	None	A Little	Some	A Lot	A Whole Lot
1. I learned more about grief and trauma reactions.	0	1	2	3	4
2. I expressed my thoughts and feelings about what happened.	0	1	2	3	4
3. I learned ways to cope when I feel upset, sad, angry, and/or stressed.	0	1	2	3	4
4. Overall, how helpful was counseling for you?	0	1	2	3	4

Has counseling been helpful or not helpful for you?

Circle: Helpful or Not helpful

If it has been helpful, how has it been helpful? Or, if it has not been helpful, why not? [Write exactly what the child states]

_____

_____

_____

_____

_____

_____

_____

_____

_____

_____

Index

Page numbers followed by 't' refer to tables.

abuse 21
activity sheets 130–74; choosing 19–20; by session 130–1; time allowed for 20, 71; unfinished 20, 91
adherence, treatment 120–1; additional meetings 129; adherence percentage 127; checklist 19, 122
adults, treatments for 104
agendas, session 19, 106–19
American Psychiatric Association (APA) 2, 3, 26
anger management: rewards for practicing 73; session 1 67; session 2 71–2; session 3 73–4
anniversaries/holidays 74
assessment tools and evaluation 36–8; additional resources 38; broad-based measures 37; First Meeting with Child: Individual Screening with Child 38, 39, 40–2; incomplete assessments 37–8; post-intervention 93; standardized measures 36–7
attention deficit hyperactivity disorder (ADHD) 20
avoidance behavior 97–9

beliefs/spirituality 11, 74–5; and answering questions 100–1
bereavement theories 4–5
bravery and hope 78, 82
breathing exercises 67, 69, 72
bullying and tension within sessions 102
burnout 26, 27, 29t

celebration in final session 92; planning 88–9, 90; vignette 104–5
certificates of program completion 89, 92
"check-ins" for teachers/staff 59–61; outline 60; protocol form 61

child abuse 21
Child Behavior Checklist 37
child safety 21
Clinical Chart 47, 79, 97; template 48
cognitive behavioral therapy 10, 11
cognitive impairments 21
co-leaders, group 47
comfort levels, increasing 66
commemoration session, vignette 104–5
commemorative rituals 103–4
community violence: child bereavement with exposure to, study 6–7; and links to PTSS, study 9–10; Survey of Children's Exposure to Community Violence 37, 46
compassion fatigue 26, 29t
complicated grief 1–2, 11, 26
complicated grief treatment (adults) 104
composition, group 47
confidentiality 66
consents 22
coping lists 86, 87
coping skills, study comparing GTI for Children with trauma narrative only and GTI for Children with 8–10
criteria for participation 20–1
cultural practices 11, 12

daydreams 78
DDWW (draw, discuss, write, witness) 12–13, 13t, 70–1
death: explaining to children 50; exposure to, assessment tool 36, 43–5; during program 103
DEC: Developmentally appropriate, Ecological perspective, Culturally relevant 10–11, 13t
depression: assessment tool 37; grief and 2, 3, 9; and suicidal thoughts 21
development of GTI for Children 5–10; study 1 5–6; study 2 6–7; study 3 7–8; study 4 8–10

Diagnostic and Statistical Manual of Mental Disorders (DSM-5): persistent complex bereavement disorder 2–3; PTSD 2–3, 26

disaster: -related grief studies 7–10; screening tool 37

domestic violence 21, 101

draw, discuss, write, witness (DDWW) 12–13, 13t, 70–1

dreams 78–9

dual process model of grief 4–5

duration of sessions 19, 22

ecological perspective 11, 28, 79

education, grief and trauma 69–70

ending: program 93; sessions 72, 83, 90

enjoyment and activities 67

environmental support 17–18

evaluation sessions 38, 91, 93; Review of Goals 37

evaluators 38

exclusions 20, 21

Experiences Survey of Having Someone Close Die 36; instructions 43–4; survey 45

facilitators meetings 22, 93

family: counseling 21, 38; support 74; therapy 20

fantasies 78

feelings, discussing 76

First Meeting with Child: Individual Screening with Child: format 38, 40–2; goals 39

framework, GTI for Children 10–12, 13t

getting ready to implement GTI for Children 17–25; abuse, neglect and domestic violence 21; criteria for participation 20–1; critical logistics 22–3, 24; environmental support 17–18; tips for facilitating sessions 19–20; using manual 19

goals 14; reviews 37, 91, 93

grief and trauma education 69–70

grief and trauma wheel 69, 102

group: composition 47; schedule 57; size 47

group model, comparing GTI individual model with GTI 7–8

Group work with adolescents after violent death 20

GTI for Children Group Schedule 57

GTI for Children Individual Schedule 58

guided imagery 79, 102

guilt, feelings of 84; dealing with expressions of 96–7

holidays/anniversaries 74

homicide, GTI studies of bereavement due to 5–6, 6–7

hope and bravery 78, 82

Hurricane Andrew 8

Hurricane Gustav 9

Hurricane Katrina 7–8, 9, 96–7, 98–9

hurricanes: avoidance behavior 98–9; feeling unsafe 101; grief studies related to 7–10; guilt about 96–7; information on 77, 86

ice breakers 66

individual model, comparing GTI group model with GTI 7–8

individual "pull-out" sessions see "pull out" sessions

individual schedule 58

literature review 1–5

logistics, critical 22–3, 24

"make up" sessions 84–5

manual, using 19

materials, resources for 23

meaning from loss, making 12, 88

meetings, pre and post clinical 31–3; post-session review 19, 31, 33; pre-session review 31, 32

memories 88, 90

missed sessions 63–4, 84, 128

Mood and Feelings Questionnaire-Child Version 37

mourning, tasks of 4

multiple violent events/deaths, dealing with 103

music 65, 69

"My Story": activity sheets 130–74; finishing 91; introducing 70; sharing with supportive adults 92, 104

narrative: activities 12–13, 13t, 70–1; completion 86; creating a coherent 80–3; first storytelling exercise 70–1; therapy 12

National Center for PTSD 38, 60

National Child Traumatic Stress Network 27, 28, 37, 38, 60

neglect 21

number of sessions 64

on-site co-ordinators/contacts 22

parental death, qualitative study of bereavement due to 5

parents and other important adults 50–8; brief personal information form 53–4; communicating with 52; GTI for Children group schedule 57; GTI for Children individual schedule 58; informing children about meetings with 68; inviting to sessions

104; meeting agenda 51–2; meeting with clinicians 50, 52, 120; post-intervention contact 93; reactions of school age children after traumatic events and losses 55–6; sharing "My Story" with 92, 104; treatments for 104

participation: criteria for 20–1; reasons for 66–7

persistent complex bereavement disorder 2–3

personal information form 53–4

play, use of 77

positive, focusing on 90

post-evaluation 93

post-session reviews 19, 31, 33

posttraumatic growth 27

posttraumatic stress disorder (PTSD): DSM-5 2–3, 26; grief associations with 2; GTI for Children studies 6, 8; measuring 37, 38; UCLA Posttraumatic Stress Disorder Index 37

posttraumatic stress symptoms (PTSS) 9–10, 97

practitioner support 26–33; mitigating negative effects of work 30t; post-session reviews 19, 31, 33; pre and post clinical meetings 31–3; pre-session reviews 31, 32; signs and symptoms of work-related stress 29t; stress and self-care 26–7; trauma-informed care 27, 28–30

pre-session reviews 31, 32

prolonged grief 2

psychiatric problems, development 3–4; risk factors for 4, 4t

"pull out" sessions 6, 83, 84–5; agenda 114; vignettes 96, 97, 99

puppets, use of 69

qualifications 38

questions: answers to clinicians' common 95, 96, 97–8, 99, 101, 103, 103–4; for creating a coherent narrative 81–2; encouraging children's 76–7; session 4 vignette 99–101; when we do not have answers, dealing with 99

reactions of school age children after traumatic events and losses 55–6

reconnecting 11, 13t, 92

relaxation 13t, 67, 69, 71–2

reminders and special items 103–4

research, current 1–5

resilience 3; GTI for Children and promotion of 11, 12, 13t

resources for materials 23

restorative retelling 11, 13t; for adults 104; techniques 81

rewards 73

risk factors for persistent distress and psychiatric problems 4, 4t

rules, session 66

safety 79; dealing with issues of 101; prioritising child 21; promoting resilience and 11, 12, 13t; session 5 vignette 101–2

screening and evaluating 36–49; assessment tools and evaluation 36–8; Clinical Chart 47–8, 79, 97; co-leaders, group 47; evaluators 38; Experiences Survey of Having Someone Close Die 36, 43–5; First Meeting with Child: Individual Screening with Child 38, 39, 40–2; group composition 47; group size 47; Violence Exposure Survey 37, 46

secondary traumatic stress 26, 27, 29t

self-reflection 27

separation distress 2

sessions, GTI for Children: additional meetings beyond 129; agendas 19, 106–19; certificates of program completion 89, 92; ending program 93; length of 19, 22; missed 63–4, 84, 128; not covering all topics in a session 95, 96; number of 64; parents/caregivers at 104; "pull out" sessions see "pull out" sessions; reminders and special items, bringing in 103–4; rules 66; summary of meetings 128; time allocation for tasks 71; tips for facilitating 19–20

sibling groups 20

size, group 47

sleep disruptions 79

space 22

special items and reminders 103–4

spirituality/beliefs 74–5, 100–1

stages of grief 4

storytelling exercise, first 70–1

Strengths and Difficulties Questionnaire 37

strengths perspective 11

stress, work-related, and self-care 26–7; measuring instruments 27; mitigating negative effects 30t; signs and symptoms 29t

suicidal children 21

supportive adults 68, 86, 92; inviting to sessions 104; sharing "My Story" 92, 104

Survey of Children's Exposure to Community Violence 37, 46

teachers/staff, education and "check-ins" 50, 59–61

teenagers, working with 20

theories supporting GTI for Children 10–12, 13t
time: allocation for tasks 20, 71; session length 19, 22; topics not covered in session 95, 96
trauma distress 2
trauma-informed care 27, 28–30
traumatic bereavement 3
traumatic grief 1, 2; assessment tools 37

UCLA Posttraumatic Stress Disorder Index 37

vicarious posttraumatic growth 27
vicarious traumatization 26, 29t; meta-analysis of studies 26–7
Violence Exposure Survey 37, 46

worksheets *see* activity sheets
worst moment 84–5
written agreement between provider and host setting 22, 24